"At a time when there is much con[...]
law of Moses, *Reading Moses, Seeing* [...]
not heat. What a helpful book for [...]
Messianic Jews. Authors Postell, Ba[...], and Sorel main[...] [...]
perspective of Torah while demonstrating its continued role of pointing to the
One of whom Moses wrote. If you want to understand the significance of the
Torah and its relationship to those who are followers of Messiah, read this out-
standing book. And while reading, keep your Bible at hand, take notes, become
enlightened and be transformed."

—**Michael Rydelnik**, Professor of Jewish Studies and Bible, Moody Bible Institute;
Syndicated Radio Host and Teacher, Open Line with Dr. Michael Rydelnik; author of
The Messianic Hope and co-editor and contributor, *The Moody Bible Commentary*

"Most Christians believe the apostle Paul's assertion to Timothy that '*all* Scripture
is inspired by God and profitable' for disciples of the Lord Jesus Christ. But how
many Christians truly study the Old Testament in their own devotions, or feel
that they really understand the differences in—and the relationship between—the
Old and New Testaments? *Reading Moses, Seeing Jesus* is a tremendous resource for
anyone interested in understanding the 'whole counsel' of Scripture, the funda-
mental purpose of the Mosaic law, the power of the Messianic prophecies, and
how to engage in effective and fruitful Jewish evangelism and discipleship. I absolutely loved this book and highly recommend it to pastors and lay people alike!"

—**Joel C. Rosenberg**, New York Times best-selling author,
Bible teacher and founder of The Joshua Fund

"We are often told that by traditional Jews that they don't need Yeshua because
they have the Torah. Yet Yeshua told the Jewish leaders of his day that, if they truly
believed Moses, they would believe in him. How can this be? The authors of this
exciting new book, written with humility and clarity, and based on solid academic
research, explain just what Yeshua meant, even demonstrating that the ultimate
goal of the Torah is to point to him. Your eyes will be opened as you read."

—**Michael L. Brown**, President, FIRE School of Ministry,
-author of *Answering Jewish Objections to Jesus* (5 vols.)

"The one most confusing issue among Messianic Jews (and today, also among
many Gentiles believers) is the role of the Torah in the life of the believer. In the
movement there are many who claim to be 'Torah observant' but fail to read the
details of what was commanded by God through Moses, and often as they claim
to keep the Torah, they are actually breaking the specific laws involved in keeping
the Torah. In the end, while they are preaching Torah, they practice grace. Thus
the publication of *Reading Moses, Seeing Jesus* is a welcome contribution to the discussion that will clearly clarify all the issues from a solid biblical perspective and
help many believers reach a biblical balance on the role and purpose of the Torah."

—**Arnold Fruchtenbaum**, Founder and Director, Ariel Ministries

"The discussion of the law and believers in Messiah has been a topic of discussion
ever since Jesus showed up and many Jews and Gentiles proclaimed him as the
fulfillment of promise. This is a brilliant little book showing Torah was not just

about law but also about the prospect of promise and the need for that Messiah. What Torah promised pointed ultimately of the need for God working from within. That message rings loud and clear in this book with an explanation to match."

—**Darrell L. Bock**, Executive Director for Cultural Engagement, Howard G. Hendricks Center for Christian Leadership and Cultural Engagement; Senior Research Professor of New Testament Studies, Dallas Theological Seminary

"Christians have discussed and debated for centuries the role of the law now that Christ has come. The authors of this delightful and clear book show that the Old Testament itself teaches that the law cannot save. Indeed, a right reading of the Old Testament points to the Messiah as the one who forgives sins, and thus Christians are oriented fundamentally to Jesus instead of the law. Here we have a biblical-theological reading of the Old Testament that is insightful and instructive, and readers will see the wonderful unity of the whole Bible in this work. I warmly welcome this contribution from Jewish believers in Jesus."

—**Thomas R. Schreiner**, James R. Buchanan Harrison Professor of New Testament, The Southern Baptist Theological Seminary

"Exegetically solid, theologically sound, contemporaneously relevant, eminently readable—all these qualifiers are true and will prove to be vindicated by its intended readership. Especially commendable—and that lends it authenticity—is the fact that its authors are Israeli scholars who embrace messianic faith that names Jesus of Nazareth as Savior and Lord. This is a must!"

—**Eugene H. Merrill**, Distinguished Professor of Old Testament Studies (Emeritus), Dallas Theological Seminary

"*Reading Moses, Seeing Jesus* is a book that will help Jews and Gentiles alike understand what it means to be a Jewish believer in Jesus, or Yeshua. Authors Seth Postell, Eitan Bar, and Erez Soref demonstrate from Scripture that to embrace Yeshua is not to abandon the Jewish people or Israel's great heritage. On the contrary, to embrace Yeshua in faith is to enter into the blessings of the new covenant prophesied by Jeremiah long ago. God has fulfilled his promises to his people Israel in the life, death, and resurrection of Yeshua the Messiah. *Reading Moses, Seeing Jesus* shows in a clear and compelling way that God has not rejected his chosen people but continues to love them and seeks to bring them into fellowship with him."

—**Craig A. Evans**, John Bisagno Distinguished Professor of Christian Origins, Houston Baptist University

"I give thanks to the Lord for the work of ONE FOR ISRAEL and Israel College of the Bible. Their book *Reading Moses, Seeing Jesus* is a rich and helpful resource for understanding the Torah both literarily and theologically, demonstrating that, by divine design, Moses indeed spoke of Yeshua (John 5:46)."

—**L. Michael Morales**, Professor of Biblical Studies, Greenville Presbyterian Theological Seminary, Taylors, SC

"As a professor and student of the Bible, I found fresh insights in this book that clarified the trajectory of the whole of Scripture. Highly recommended!"

—**George H. Guthrie**, Professor of New Testament, Regent College, Vancouver, BC

HOW THE TORAH FULFULLS ITS GOAL IN YESHUA

Expanded Second Edition

Seth D. Postell • Eitan Bar • Erez Soref

ISRAEL COLLEGE OF THE BIBLE

WEAVER BOOK
COMPANY
WOOSTER, OHIO

Reading Moses, Seeing Jesus: How the Torah Fulfills Its Purpose in Yeshua

Copyright © 2017 Seth D. Postell, Eitan Bar, Erez Soref, and Michelle Shelfer

Published by
ONE FOR ISRAEL Ministry and
Weaver Book Company
1190 Summerset Dr.
Wooster, OH 44691
Visit us at weaverbookcompany.com

Cover design: Ruth Winkler
Interior Design: Nicholas Richardson

Print: 978-1-941337-91-2

Library of Congress Cataloging-in-Publication Data
A CIP catalogue record for this book is available from the Library of Congress.

Printed in the United States of America

This book is lovingly dedicated
to all people who have a zeal for God,
but not according to knowledge.
(Rom. 10:2–4)

Contents

Preface

We decided to write this short book because questions about the believer's relationship to the Torah (the five Books of Moses, or the Pentateuch) and its commandments (the Law) are among the top five most frequently asked questions on the ONE FOR ISRAEL FAQ list. Since Jesus kept the Law, are believers (Jewish and Gentile) also obliged to keep the Law, or at least some portions of it (Sabbath, the food laws, etc.)? What about the Oral Law (rabbinic traditions)? How does the Torah point to the Messiah? How do we apply the Law of Moses today? Though this book is based on at least a decade of academic research, it is written with the non-academic reader in mind. Our goal is to provide easy-to-understand answers to the questions related to the Torah, and to do so in a manner thoroughly rooted in a careful reading of the biblical text.

Dr. Seth Postell (PhD in Hebrew Bible) is the Academic Dean at ONE FOR ISRAEL's Bible College (Israel College of the Bible). Eitan Bar (DMin) is ONE FOR ISRAEL's Director of Media and Evangelism. Dr. Erez Soref (PhD in psychology) is the President of ONE FOR ISRAEL \ Israel College of the Bible. Seth, Eitan, and Erez are all Jewish Israeli believers in Yeshua (Jesus).

We truly hope this little book will stimulate your thinking and challenge you to deepen your appreciation for the person and work of Yeshua by meditating on the Torah day and night (Josh. 1:8; Ps. 1:2–3).

Our Unique Terminology

We as authors of this work are influenced by our Jewish surroundings, heritage, and culture, leading us to use terms that may be unfamiliar to some of our readers. Our intent is not to exclude or alienate, but simply to use the linguistic touchstones that make sense in the context of who we are and how we think. In this work you will find a focus on the Hebrew nuances of words from Scripture, references to historical Jewish scholars and their writings (not necessarily biblical), and a general appeal to read through Jewish eyes, as we reveal textual connections in the hopes that this will deepen insight into the meaning of the story being told in the Torah.

We have tried to be very consistent in our use of the terms "Torah" and "Law." When we use the term "Torah," we are referring to the five Books of Moses as a whole (the Pentateuch). When we use the word "Law," we are referring specifically to the commandments given to Israel. The only exception is when we use quotations from the English Standard Version (ESV). In some cases, the ESV uses "Law" (capital L) to refer to the five Books of Moses as a whole (Matt. 5:17; 22:40; Luke 16:16; 2:24; Acts 13:15). In other cases, "Law" (capital L) is restricted to the commandments of the Sinai covenant (Matt. 12:5; Luke 2:22, 24; Gal. 3:10) and sometimes "law" (lowercase l) refers to the commandments of Sinai (Matt. 23:23; Acts 13:39; 15:5; 21:24; Rom. 2:12). In Romans 3:21, "Law" (capital L) refers to the five Books of Moses and "law" (lowercase l) refers to the commandments of Sinai. The ESV is clearly not consistent. Though we quote from the ESV, our understanding of these terms will be quite clear by the context in which we quote the verse.

Law (capital L): the commandments of the Sinai covenant.
Maimonides (Rambam): a twelfth-century Jewish philosopher who is
   perhaps the most influential thinker and writer on the Talmud.

(Not to be confused with thirteenth-century scholar Torah
scholar Ramban, or Nachmanides.)

Oral Law: the rabbinic traditions.

Rashi: the most famous Jewish Bible commentator.

Talmud: a collection of ancient traditional, non-biblical Jewish writings comprised of rabbinic commentary on the Law of Moses.

Tanakh: The Hebrew Scriptures, also known as the Old Testament, made up of the Torah, the Prophets (Nevi'im), and the Writings (Ketuvim).

Torah: the Pentateuch in its entirety—that is, the five Books of Moses.

Yeshua: The Jewish name for Jesus.

Acknowledgements

We wish to thank a number of people for "birthing" this book. Special thanks go to the following people who invested much time and thought in the evolution of this book from the first to the current edition of the manuscript: Jim Sibley, Esther Martin, Joseph Boone, Lynn Rosenberg, Jo Blower, David Hecht, and Wes Taber. We also wish to thank several people who carefully interacted with the content: Dominick Hernandez, Jeffery Seif, Jeffery Cranford, Boaz Michael, Winn Crenshaw, Ron Seabrooke, Dave Brodsky, Ty Flewelling, George Guthrie, Mitch Glaser, and Yoel Seton. We are especially thankful to Michelle Shelfer, a truly gifted editor who worked night and day to make this expanded edition a reality. We also want to express our appreciation for Jim Weaver, who made the publication of this book possible. Finally, we want to express our gratitude to John Sailhamer, may his memory be blessed, who demonstrated in the classroom and in writing that the Torah is fearfully and wonderfully made!

Introduction

We open this book with the honest confession of three Israeli Jewish followers of Yeshua (Jesus). Being Jewish is not easy! Being a Jewish follower of Yeshua is even more difficult. As Jews, we have to deal with growing anti-Semitism worldwide. As messianic Jews, we are often rejected by our own families. Spiritual leaders in the Jewish community tell us that we are no longer Jewish if we believe in "that man." Within the body of Messiah we are often misunderstood by our Gentile brothers and sisters who may not have a clue about our acute identity struggles—struggles that Gentile believers typically do not have to face.

The early church wrestled with identity issues from a completely different perspective. Since the messianic faith was Jewish, the challenge came when Gentiles were added to the early messianic community. The very first church council (Acts 15) dealt with how Gentiles fit into an essentially Jewish faith and culture. They concluded that Gentile believers do not have to keep the Law (though many Gentile Christians today are sincerely wondering whether or not their love for the Jewish Savior ought to be expressed by observing the Law).

But then what about Jewish believers in Yeshua today? Doesn't Acts 15 assume that Jewish believers will continue keeping the Law?[1] Paul goes out of his way in Acts 21:23–24 to prove once and for all that he lives "in observance of the law." Yeshua declares that "whoever relaxes one of the least of these commandments and teaches others to do the same will be called least in the kingdom of heaven,

---

1. Any argument from silence in favor of obligatory messianic Jewish Law observance must not ignore Peter's clear, rather shocking confession in Acts 15:10: "Now, therefore, why are you putting God to the test by placing a yoke on the neck of the disciples that neither our fathers nor we have been able to bear?" (All Scripture references, unless otherwise noted, are taken from the English Standard Version [ESV].)

but whoever does them and teaches them will be called great in the kingdom of heaven" (Matt. 5:19).[2] Our Messiah tells us to "do and observe whatever they [the scribes and the Pharisees] tell you"—the Law along with the rabbis' oral interpretation of it (Matt. 23:2–3). Moses tells us the commandments of the Law are eternal (see, e.g., Exod. 12:14, 17, 24; 27:21; 28:43; 29:9, 28; 30:21; 31:16).[3] Case closed! Jewish believers, in obedience to our Rabbi Yeshua and our teacher Moses, and by following the example of Paul, must obey the Law as good and faithful messianic Jews.

Though the logic of the previous paragraph is compelling, we are still faced with a big interpretive dilemma. Why? Because as clear as those passages may seem, other passages in the New Testament lead us to believe that we are no longer "under the Law." For instance, the apostle Paul tells us the Law was added to earlier promises made by God, not to replace those promises but simply to guide us as a tutor who will lead us to the Messiah (see Gal. 3:1–24). But now that the Messiah has come, we are "no longer under a guardian" (Gal. 3:25). In addition, Paul says, "Therefore let no one pass judgment on you in questions of food and drink, or with regard to a festival or a new moon or a Sabbath. These are a shadow of the things to come, but the substance belongs to Christ" (Col. 2:16–17). The writer of Hebrews makes very clear the fact that Yeshua's priesthood necessitates a change in the Law, since He is not a descendant of Aaron, and not even from the priestly tribe of Levi: "For when there is a change in the priesthood, there is necessarily a change in the law as well" (Heb.

---

2. Yeshua actually explains what Matthew 5:17–20 means in the rest of the chapter. It is clear that people were accusing Yeshua and his followers of abolishing the Law. But, true followers of Yeshua have standards that go beyond the written demands of the Law; He raised the bar higher! For example, Messiah's followers will keep the commandment prohibiting adultery, because they will not even allow themselves to look lustfully at a woman. It is quite evident by Yeshua's teachings on adultery that Yeshua did not relax the commandments of the Law.

3. It should be noted that the word typically translated "eternal" (*olam*) is sometimes used to express a lengthy, though limited, period of time. A good example of this is found in Jeremiah 25:9. God says that he will make the Land of Israel an "eternal desolation." Yet in Jeremiah 29:10, God promises to bring his people back to the Land seventy years later. In this case, *olam* refers to a period of seventy years. Therefore, one cannot argue that the Law must be kept eternally simply because of the phrase "eternal statute."

7:12). He goes on to tell us that the system of worship prescribed by the Law is a copy and a shadow of better, more perfect things (Heb. 8:5; 10:1), the purpose of which is to point us to a better covenant since the former covenant "disappeared" (became obsolete) with the making of the new covenant (Heb. 8:6–13).[4]

A first step toward some kind of consensus on this subject involves humbly and honestly acknowledging that there would be no argument about the role of the Law among believers if the issues were simple and straightforward. The fact of the matter is that interpretation is not a science, though we typically try to explain (and even explain away) statements in the Bible contrary to our position. There will continue to be believers on both sides of this issue, who struggle to understand why those on the other side do not see the "obvious truth" in the matter.

We want to begin by expressing our genuine appreciation for healthy and respectful disagreement. We realize that not everyone will agree with what we have to say about the meaning of the Torah and the purpose of the Law in the Torah. We would not have written this book if we believed that everything had already been said on the matter. We believe this book offers a unique contribution to the discussion.

Many people read the Torah through the lens of rabbinic Judaism, in which the Torah is understood to be a law book: to follow the Torah is to keep the commandments of the Sinai covenant. We disagree with this common assumption. Rather, our thesis about the

---

4. What does the author of Hebrews mean by "becoming obsolete and growing old" and "ready to vanish away" in Hebrews 8:13? Though some have taken the timing of the actual "vanishing away" of the old covenant to be future to the time of the writing of Hebrews, this does not appear to be the author's point. The author is likely referring to the implications of the word "new" at the time when Jeremiah the prophet wrote, "I will make a new covenant." When Jeremiah called the covenant a "new covenant" (Jer. 31:31) on the eve of the destruction of the first temple, he was saying that the old covenant was already becoming obsolete and "ready to vanish away" in his day. This suggests that the old covenant became obsolete and vanished when the new covenant was made. We have purposely written "disappeared" and "obsolete" because that is precisely the point being made in the text: when the new covenant was made through the shedding of Messiah's blood, the old covenant disappeared and became obsolete.

purpose of the Torah (Genesis through Deuteronomy) is that it is an historical narrative, whose purpose is to lead Israel *through* the broken Law and beyond, namely, *to* the Messiah who, Moses assures his readers, will come in the last days. To be faithful followers of the Torah, in our view, is to believe in Yeshua (see John 5:39–47). We defend this thesis by looking at several key passages in the Torah.

In chapter 1, we look at the Torah's introduction (Gen. 1–11) and conclusion (Deut. 29–34). By looking at the Torah's beginning and ending, we see that Moses prophesied Israel's future breaking of the Law and subsequent exile before they entered the Promised Land, suggesting that his *primary* purpose for writing the Torah could not have been to lead Israel *to*, but rather *through* the broken Law and beyond.

In chapter 2, we look at the account of the giving of the Law at Mount Sinai (Exod. 19:1–Num. 10:10) situated between the Wilderness Narratives leading *to* (Exod. 15:22–18:27), and then *away from* (Num. 10:11–36:13), Mount Sinai. We see a direct relationship between the giving of the Law and a breakdown of Israel's faith, the result of which is death (see Rom. 7:9–10). This textual data provides yet more evidence that Moses' purpose for writing the Torah could not have been simply to lead us *to* the Law, but rather *through* the Law and beyond.

In chapter 3, we demonstrate where the Torah is aiming, if not toward the Law: it is aiming toward the Messiah. We look at passages that speak about "the last days." We argue that these passages reveal the ultimate goal for which Moses wrote the Torah, namely, to bring us *through* Israel's breaking of the Law and *to* the Messiah in the last days.

Chapter 4 introduces the *creation mandate*, God's pattern of blessing that is played out in the story of Adam and Eve. We see Adam as God's first and prototypical king and priest, illuminating his creation purposes for humanity.

Chapter 5 takes us to the rivers of Babylon. Adam experiences the consequences of his disobedience in the form of an eastward exile, which is a prefiguring of Israel's later exile. How can Adam/ Israel overcome their disobedience and be restored to God's intended blessings?

Chapters 6 through 8 take us through three selected poetic speeches in the Torah that reveal how the creation mandate will finally be restored through a special individual from a specific lineage who will crush the head of his enemy.

Chapter 9 answers the question, Why then the Law? (Gal 3:19) by bringing to light six prevailing functions of the Law: Law as tutor, shadow, theology, love, wisdom, and prosecuting attorney.

Chapter 10 gives us a way of understanding the archaic, sometimes bizarre laws that we encounter among the 613 commandments given at Mt. Sinai.

This brings us to chapter 11, where we encounter the impossibility of keeping the Law of Moses. We look at how it became impossible to keep, and how the rabbinical sages responded to this national identity crisis, giving particular attention to the "Oral Law."

In chapter 12 we look at what it means to be a messianic Jew and our relationship to the Law and to Jewish tradition. The conclusion summarizes our findings and offer a final challenge to the reader.

Before we formally begin our study, let us state quite clearly the purpose of this book. First, we wrote this book to provide an answer for questions about the believer's relationship to the Law. With the rapid growth of the messianic movement since the early 1970s, more and more believers are realizing two simple, yet profoundly world-shaking facts—fact 1: Jesus is Jewish; fact 2: we cannot understand the New Testament without carefully studying the Old Testament. These two discoveries have resulted in a growing number of believers, both Jewish and Gentile, who struggle with questions about their relationship to the Law.

Second, we wrote this book to show how Yeshua is the Torah's goal. For some people, a few verses in the New Testament suffice. "For if you believed Moses, you would believe me; for he wrote of me" (John 5:46). "For Christ is the end [goal] of the law for righteousness to everyone who believes" (Rom. 10:4). While we affirm the truth of these verses, we believe it is incumbent upon every believer to examine the Scriptures daily to see how these things are so (Acts 17:11). To say that Jesus is the goal of the Torah is one thing, but to prove it from the Torah is entirely another matter.

There are only a handful of messianic prophecies in the Torah (Gen. 3:15; 49:8-12; Num. 24:7-9, 17-19; Deut. 18:15). If our conclusions about the Torah's goal were a matter of mathematics, we could easily conclude that the Law is the purpose of the Torah, since references to the Messiah are few and far between, while verses referring to the Law occupy roughly half of all the verses in the Torah. However, from beginning to end a singular story is told in the Torah, not just in a smattering of verses but woven into its very fabric. Perhaps by examining the narrative structure of the Torah with its many parallel story lines and recurring themes we may see signposts pointing consistently and undeniably toward the Messiah and our need for Him.

All are welcome here. We hope readers of this work will include those who believe that Yeshua is the promised Messiah, both Jewish and Gentile, and those who do not share that belief, both Jewish and Gentile, and that for all readers it will be a journey of discovery. It is our sincere expectation that by the end of this book, you will have sufficient and satisfying evidence for proclaiming with Phillip and with the writers of this book: "We have found him of whom Moses in the Law and also the prophets wrote, Jesus of Nazareth, the son of Joseph" (John 1:45).

CHAPTER 1

The Torah Anticipates Lawbreaking

Through New Testament Eyes

Paul states in Romans 10:4 that the Messiah is the goal of the Torah: "For Christ is the end of the law for righteousness to everyone who believes."[1] In John 5:46, Yeshua argues that since the religious leaders do not believe Moses, they do not accept Him as the promised Messiah. "For if you believed Moses, you would believe me; for he wrote of me." Likewise, in Matthew 5:17 Yeshua says, "Do not think that I have come to abolish the Law or the Prophets;[2] I have not come to abolish them but to fulfill them."[3]

---

1. There is some debate whether or not the word *telos* should be translated as the end of the Law (i.e., for establishing righteousness) or the goal (i.e., the intended destination of the Law). Though the context appears to support the latter interpretation, both interpretations have merit.

2. In the context, Yeshua is referring to the Torah as a whole and not just to the Law. This is clearly the case because of the way in which He places "the Law" side by side with "the Prophets."

3. Some in the Hebrew roots movement attempt to back-translate the Greek into Yeshua's mother-tongue in order to understand, not the verbal meaning of the Greek text but the "real" meaning behind the Greek text. By appealing to this logic, some would argue that Yeshua did not come to "fulfill" the Torah, but to "interpret it properly." There are two very serious flaws with this school of thought. First, it is notoriously difficult to back-translate Koine Greek into Hebrew and/or Aramaic. Any and every back-translation will always remain at the level of conjecture. A second flaw resulting from the first has to do with the authority of the biblical text. When our understanding of the biblical text rests in a conjectural back-translation, the authority of God's word no longer rests in the biblical text, but in the scholars who provide the back-translation. The Gospel of John clearly teaches that God gave his Spirit to the disciples after Yeshua's ascension to teach

The author of Hebrews argues that the Law was never a goal in and of itself, but rather it prescribed a system of worship that was divinely intended to point people to the Messiah. He writes about the tabernacle,

> By this the Holy Spirit indicates that the way into the holy places is not yet opened as long as the first section is still standing (which is symbolic for the present age). According to this arrangement, gifts and sacrifices are offered that cannot perfect the conscience of the worshiper, but deal only with food and drink and various washings, regulations for the body imposed until the time of reformation. (Heb. 9:8–10; see also 10:1)

The New Testament teaches that the Messiah is the goal and fulfillment of the Torah as a whole and the Law in particular. How did Yeshua, Paul and the author of Hebrews come to such conclusions? Are their conclusions based on the grammatical-historical interpretation of the Torah,[4] or can one only arrive at such interpretations by reading the Torah through the lens of the New Testament writings? These questions are particularly relevant when we consider that verses about the Messiah in the Torah represent less than a half of one percent of all the verses in the Torah! We believe the authors of the New Testament did not impose added meaning on the Torah but actually understood the original meaning intended by Moses when he wrote the Torah (called "exegesis").[5]

---

them "all things and bring to [their] remembrance all that [He] said to [them]" (John 14:26; see 2:22; 12:16; 20:9). Because the disciples were uniquely anointed by God's Spirit to preserve Yeshua's teachings, their translation of Yeshua's words into Greek was inspired and therefore completely authoritative and reliable for faith and practice.

4. That is, the literal interpretation of the meaning intended by the original author.

5. Exegesis is the process of interpretation whereby the reader seeks after the grammatical-historical meaning of a text, more specifically, the meaning intended by the text's historical author.

The Deeds of the Fathers Are a Sign to the Sons

If the ultimate purpose of the Torah is to provide Israel with the Law and to motivate them to keep it, we should expect to find some indication of this aim in its introduction and conclusion (Gen. 1–11; Deut. 29–34), since introductions and conclusions in biblical literature typically contain the major themes and purpose of entire books.

In order to understand the purpose and meaning of Genesis 1–11 and its function as the introduction to the Torah, let's look at a common literary feature in the Genesis narratives. It is described by the rabbis as *"ma'asei avot, siman l'banim,"* meaning "the deeds of the fathers are a sign to the sons." *Ma'asei avot, siman l'banim* means Moses wrote stories about the patriarchs not only to tell us about the patriarchs (and about those who preceded them) but also to tell us what would happen to the descendants of those patriarchs (i.e., the nation of Israel) in the future. Though some scholars use this Hebrew phrase, others identify this literary feature as narrative typology or literary analogy (an English name we prefer to use). Though some may accuse us of deferring to allegorical interpretations to reach our conclusions about the meaning of the stories in the Torah, this is not the case. Literary analogy is a tangible, identifiable feature in the text itself and was recognized by ancient and modern interpreters, Jewish and Christian alike. There are also commonly accepted and recognized criteria for making the claim that one text was intentionally written as an analogy, or foreshadowing, of another text: (1) shared words and phrases (lexical parallels); and (2) shared plot (thematic parallels).[6]

For example, the Torah's description of Israel's exodus in Genesis 43:1–Exodus 12:38 repeats key words, phrases, and themes found elsewhere only in Genesis 12:10–13:2. This suggests that Israel's exodus is intentionally described to remind the reader of what happened to Abram. In both accounts, we find (1) "heavy famine" (Gen. 12:10; 43:1); (2) descent to Egypt (Gen. 12:10; 46:6); (3) a

---

6. We also make use of a third criterion, namely, the history of interpretation. In other words, it is extremely helpful to find others in the history of interpretation who recognize how one story foreshadows another, or how one story is written in the light of an earlier story.

life-threatening situation to the males but not to the females (Gen. 12:12; Exod. 1:16); (4) "captivity" in Pharaoh's service (Gen. 12:15; Exod. 1:11); (5) plagues upon the Egyptians (Gen. 12:17; Exod. 7–12); (6) expulsion from Egypt because of the plagues (Gen. 12:20; Exod. 12:33); and (7) the departure from Egypt with great wealth (Gen. 12:16; 13:2; Exod. 12:35, 38). The story of Abram and Sarai's sojourn in Egypt due to a great famine, God's striking of Pharaoh's house with plagues, and their "exodus" from Egypt with great riches (Gen. 12:10–13:2) reveals not only what happened to Abram and Sarai but also prefigures what will happen to Israel over 400 years later (Gen. 43:1–Exod. 12:38).

Another example of a literary analogy (*ma'asei avot*) is the story of Noah, a figure who intentionally foreshadows Moses. While English readers of the Bible know that God saved Noah and his family from a watery death by means of an ark (*tevah* in Hebrew; Gen. 6:14), some may be surprised to learn that Moses was also saved from a water death in an ark (*tevah* in Hebrew; Exod. 2:3, 5). Though the ESV translates *tevah* in Exodus 2:3 and 5 as "basket," this is clearly an exception since every other time *tevah* is found in the Torah it means "ark" (Gen. 6:14–16, 18–19; 7:1, 7, 9, 13, 15, 17–18, 23; 8:1, 4, 6, 9–10, 13, 16, 19; 9:10, 18). Moreover, every other time the word "basket" appears in the ESV, a different Hebrew word is used. In Genesis-Numbers, the Hebrew word for basket is *sal* (Gen. 40:17; Exod. 29:3, 23, 32; Lev. 8:2, 26, 31; Num. 6:15, 17, 19), and in Deuteronomy the word is *tene* (Deut. 26:2, 4; 28:5, 17). Why would Moses avoid the two proper Hebrew words for basket in favor of a word only used elsewhere to refer to Noah's ark if not to make an intentional link between the two stories? This link appears all the more intentional when we consider that in both stories the arks are waterproofed (Gen. 6:14; Exod. 2:3), and these arks serve to protect the main characters from drowning. Remarkably, only Noah and Moses receive architectural blueprints for redemptively significant structures from God (Gen. 6:14–16; Exod. 25–31). Noah's importance in God's redemptive purposes (Gen. 5:29) intentionally prefigures Moses' role as Israel's redeemer (Exod. 3:10).

Just as Abram's sojourn in Egypt and Noah's rescue from the waters of death are written as signs of later events, likewise the story of Adam and Eve is written with Israel's future in mind.[7] In other words, by reading about Adam, we can also know what will happen to Israel in the future. So with Israel in mind, we look at the general story line of the first three chapters of Genesis.

From Adam and Eve to Israel

In Genesis 1:28, God (1) *blesses* Adam and Eve and (2) tells them to be *fruitful* and (3) tells them to subdue (conquer) the *land*.[8] Notice the major elements of God's promises to Abraham (Gen. 12:1–3)—blessing, seed, and land—contained in this verse. Later in Genesis, God's promises to Abraham and his descendants include all three aspects of this *creation mandate:* blessing, seed, and the conquest of the land (Gen. 14:18–15:18; 26:2–4; 35:9–12; see also Exod. 1:7; Num. 32:22, 29).

In Genesis 2, God prepares a very special land (garden) for Adam and then brings him into it. Adam's continued enjoyment of this garden is contingent upon the keeping of just a few commandments: "be fruitful," "subdue the land," and "do not eat from the tree of the knowledge of good and evil" (Gen. 1:28; 2:17). In Genesis 3, we are introduced to the serpent, an "inhabitant" of the garden who deceives Adam and Eve. Adam and Eve should have subdued the serpent (Gen. 1:28), but instead are themselves subdued by the serpent, disobey God's commandment, and are subsequently exiled from the garden, eastward, where their descendants eventually find themselves in Babylon (Gen. 11:2, 9).

Does this story sound familiar? Adam's story becomes Israel's story in Joshua through Kings. God blesses Israel and makes them fruitful. He gives them not a few, but 613 commandments. He brings them to the land of Canaan in order to subdue it and to conquer its inhabitants. Their presence in the land is contingent on keeping the Law. Like Adam, they break the commandments and are exiled eastward to Babylon.

---

7. As recorded in the biblical text.

8. The Hebrew word for land, *eretz*, most commonly translated in Genesis 1:28 as "world," is most frequently translated as "land" in the English translations of the Torah. For example, *eretz* is used 845 times in the Torah; 159 times the ESV translates the word as "earth," 642 times as "land."

If the ultimate purpose of Genesis 1–11 is to both encourage and to warn Israel to keep the Law, it is difficult to see how this introduction achieves that goal. Adam and Eve live in a perfect world. Their continued presence in the garden is contingent on the keeping of only a few commandments, not 613 commandments. Under the best conditions this world has ever seen, Adam and Eve break the only "do not" law they are given and consequently die in exile. It is not at all clear how the telling of the story of Adam and Eve's failure to keep one of only a few commandments in a perfect world is supposed to encourage Israel to keep 613 commandments in a fallen world. Actually, it offers no encouragement at all! And if we consider the principle of "deeds of the fathers as a sign to the sons" (*ma'asei avot, siman l'banim*), Adam's story *never was intended* to warn Israel from following in Adam's footsteps (i.e., a warning to keep the Law). Rather, Adam's story *is intended to be* a prophecy that Israel will follow in Adam's footsteps. "Israel, you will be just like Adam. You will enter the land, be tempted by the Canaanites to follow their ways, you will break the Law, and then you will be exiled!"[9]

The End Echoes the Beginning

When we look at the conclusion of the Torah (Deut. 29–34), we see exactly the same perspective that we find in the introduction. Moses does not expect Israel to keep the Law. Rather, he predicts Israel will break the Law and go into exile.

In Moses' forty years with Israel in the wilderness, he experiences Israel breaking the Sinai covenant the moment it was made (Exod. 32), as well as continuous complaining (Exod. 15:24; 16:2, 7–8; 17:3; Num. 11:1; 14:2, 27, 29, 36; 16:11; 17:5, 10), and unbelief (Num. 14:11; 20:12; Deut. 1:32; 9:23). These experiences lead him to the conclusion that Israel's enjoyment of the land will be short-lived. In the

---

9. Someone might object to our position by arguing the absurdity of God giving the Law to Israel if he knew they would break it before he gave it. This same argument, however, just as easily applies to God's commandments to Adam and Eve in the garden. Of course, God knew Adam and Eve would break his commandments before he gave them. Likewise, God knew Israel would worship a golden calf before he brought them out of Egypt. God's gracious plan to save the world did not begin when humankind disobeyed. Rather, God planned to redeem the world by means of the Lamb before the foundation of the world (Rev. 13:8).

conclusion of the Torah, Moses prophesies that Israel will assuredly repeat Adam's story by breaking the Sinai covenant and being exiled.

And when all these things come upon you, the blessing and the curse, which I have set before you, and you call them to mind among all the nations where the LORD your God has driven you. (Deut. 30:1)

And the LORD said to Moses, "Behold, you are about to lie down with your fathers. Then this people will rise and whore after the foreign gods among them in the land that they are entering, and they will forsake me and break my covenant that I have made with them. Then my anger will be kindled against them in that day, and I will forsake them and hide my face from them, and they will be devoured. And many evils and troubles will come upon them, so that they will say in that day, 'Have not these evils come upon us because our God is not among us?' And I will surely hide my face in that day because of all the evil that they have done, because they have turned to other gods. Now therefore write this song and teach it to the people of Israel. Put it in their mouths, that this song may be a witness for me against the people of Israel. For when I have brought them into the land flowing with milk and honey, which I swore to give to their fathers, and they have eaten and are full and grown fat, they will turn to other gods and serve them, and despise me and break my covenant. And when many evils and troubles have come upon them, this song shall confront them as a witness (for it will live unforgotten in the mouths of their offspring). For I know what they are inclined to do even today, before I have brought them into the land that I swore to give." (Deut. 31:16–21)

He made him ride on the high places of the land, and he ate the produce of the field, and he suckled him with honey out of the rock, and oil out of the flinty rock. Curds from the herd, and milk from the flock, with fat of lambs, rams of

Bashan and goats, with the very finest of the wheat—and you drank foaming wine made from the blood of the grape. But Jeshurun grew fat, and kicked; you grew fat, stout, and sleek; then he forsook God who made him and scoffed at the Rock of his salvation. They stirred him to jealousy with strange gods; with abominations they provoked him to anger. They sacrificed to demons that were no gods, to gods they had never known, to new gods that had come recently, whom your fathers had never dreaded. You were unmindful of the Rock that bore you, and you forgot the God who gave you birth. The LORD saw it and spurned them, because of the provocation of his sons and his daughters. And he said, "I will hide my face from them; I will see what their end will be, for they are a perverse generation, children in whom is no faithfulness. They have made me jealous with what is no god; they have provoked me to anger with their idols. So I will make them jealous with those who are no people; I will provoke them to anger with a foolish nation. (Deut. 32:13–21)

The fact that Moses so clearly prophesies Israel's disobedience and exile at the end of the Torah strongly suggests that Adam's story is written with Israel's future disobedience in mind.

Failure Is Assured

Some might object by pointing to the numerous times Moses calls Israel to keep the Law. How do we reconcile Moses' pleas to Israel to keep the Law on the one hand, with his prophecies that Israel will not keep the Law on the other? Perhaps an analogy to this tension between a call for obedience and the certainty of disobedience can be found in Jeremiah. Jeremiah assumes Israel's failure to heed the prophet's numerous warnings to keep the Law throughout the book (Jer. 1:1–3). For instance, Jeremiah implores Israel to keep the Sabbath or else Jerusalem will be burned (Jer. 17:21–22, 24, 27). But the book of Jeremiah also makes it clear that Israel does not obey, and so we read about Jerusalem's destruction by fire at the end of the book (Jer. 52:13). Jeremiah's consistent warnings to keep the Law, found throughout the book and which are given prior to the exile, coupled with Israel's failure and exile at the end of the book, help bring its message and its theology more clearly into focus. The ultimate purpose of the book of Jeremiah is not to get Israel to keep the Law so they will not be exiled. The ultimate purpose is to tell us how God will graciously save Israel in spite of their disobedience, through the Messiah and the new covenant (Jer. 30–33). It is in this light that we more clearly appreciate the Torah's ultimate goal as well. Israel is repeatedly told to keep the Law and is promised blessings for obedience, but God graciously and unconditionally promises to bless Israel through the coming Messiah in spite of the certainty of their failure.

Since the Torah's introduction and conclusion take for granted, prophetically speaking, Israel's disobedience to the Law, it hardly makes sense to suggest that the Torah's purpose is to encourage Israel to keep the Law. The Torah's ultimate goal must be conceived, not in terms of bringing Israel *to* the Law but rather in terms of leading Israel *through* the broken Law, through the violated covenant and beyond.

CHAPTER 2

Failure of Faith Leads to Death

If the goal of the Torah is the Law, why does Moses strategically highlight Israel's unbelief and death after the giving of the Law? The apostle Paul writes, "For the law brings wrath, but where there is no law there is no transgression" (Rom. 4:15). In 2 Corinthians 3:6–7, he calls the Sinai covenant a "ministry of death." In Romans 10:3–8, Paul speaks of a righteousness based on the Law, which is opposed to a righteousness based on faith.

How could Paul make such statements? The answer is straightforward: by meditating on the Torah. The solution to understanding Paul's use of the Torah is to begin with a close reading of the Torah itself. Often, believers think they can understand the Tanakh (i.e., the Hebrew Scriptures) only through the New Testament writings. We believe this equation should be reversed: only when we have given careful attention to the meaning of the Tanakh can we understand the New Testament writings.

As we now look at the story of the giving of the Law (Exod. 19:1–Num. 10:10) in its larger literary context, we will point out two quite surprising details in the text. First, Israel's experience with God at Mount Sinai does not achieve its stated purpose, namely, a response of faith. Second, Israel's transgression, after the Law is given, results in death.

Trying to get our arms around a book the size of the Torah is not a simple task. It is helpful to think of the Torah as one very big narrative, from the creation of the universe to Moses' death on Mount Nebo, comprised of six major time periods or narrative sections:[1]

1. The Primeval History (Gen. 1–11)
2. The Patriarchal Narrative (Gen. 12–50)
3. The Exodus Narrative (Exod. 1:1–15:21)
4. The Wilderness Narratives *to* (Exod. 15:22–18:27) and *from* (Num. 10:11–36:13) Mount Sinai[2]
5. The Sinai Narrative (Exod. 19:1–Num. 10:10)
6. Moses' exposition of the Torah in the land of Moab (Deut. 1–34)

Righteous Faith and Faithless Grumbling

When we read through the Torah, we see that faith, though not mentioned frequently, is mentioned strategically in terms of the structure of the Torah as a whole.[3] In all but the first narrative section (Gen. 1–11), the phrase "to believe" appears at key moments in the plot of the story.[4] Those key moments tell us a great deal.

In arguably the single most important part of the Patriarchal Narrative, the making of the Abrahamic covenant, we find the famous verse about Abraham's faith (Gen. 15:6) sandwiched between God's promise of a seed (Gen. 15:1–5) and of the land (Gen. 15:7–18). "And he believed the LORD, and he counted it to him as righteousness."

The following section, the Exodus Narrative (Exod. 1:1–15:21), begins and ends with Israel's faith. When Moses and Aaron first

---

1. Our division of the Torah into larger narrative sections is generally recognized and based on tangible features in the literary structure of the Torah.

2. Though the Wilderness Narratives to and from Mount Sinai represent, in one sense, two different narrative sections, their role as the literary framework for the Sinai Narrative compels us to consider their purpose as a unity.

3. John H. Sailhamer, *Pentateuch as Narrative* (Grand Rapids: Zondervan, 1992), 59–62.

4. Though faith is not mentioned in the Primeval Narrative (Gen. 1–11), Moses does highlight the fact that Enoch and Noah "walked with God" (Gen. 5:22, 24; 6:9). This faith-walk is later used to describe the life of Abraham (Gen. 13:17; 17:1; 24:40). Enoch and Noah's "walk" with God rescues them from death (though only temporarily in Noah's case), and provides an occasion to highlight Noah's righteousness (Gen. 6:9).

assemble the elders and sons of Israel in Egypt to reveal God's plan, we are told that the people "believed" (Exod. 4:31) and bowed their heads and worshiped. Likewise, at the end of the Exodus Narrative and before the whole assembly sings their song of praise (Exod. 15), we see that the people's reaction to the miraculous crossing of the Red Sea is faith. "Israel saw the great power that the LORD used against the Egyptians, so the people feared the LORD, and they believed in the LORD and in his servant Moses" (Exod. 14:31).

It is worth making a few comments about the next narrative section, the Wilderness Narrative *to* Mount Sinai (Exod. 15:22–18:27), though we will return to this section later to compare it with Israel's journey away *from* Mount Sinai. Here we see how Israel's experiences with God in Egypt fail to make a lasting impression. After God reveals his miraculous powers over the waters of the Red Sea, Israel faithlessly complains about a lack of water (Exod. 15:22–27). Though Israel's complaining continues unabated until they reach Mount Sinai (Exod. 15:24; 16:2, 7–8; 17:3), God patiently and graciously leads them victoriously past the Amalekites into his thunderous presence. Faith is surprisingly absent in this section, however.[5]

The next reference to faith is found in the introduction to the fifth and largest narrative section in the Torah, the Sinai Narrative (Exod. 19:1–Num. 10:10). The moment has come for the Law to be given; the Lord will appear to the people in a new and dramatic way. And now we see that faith is the response God himself desires from Israel when they encounter Him on the mountain: "And the LORD said to Moses, 'Behold, I am coming to you in a thick cloud, that the people may hear when I speak with you, and may also believe you forever'" (Exod. 19:9).[6] Here God explains to Moses quite explicitly the purpose for his dramatic appearance to Israel on Mount Sinai: that the

---

5. The absence of the faith theme in the Wilderness Narrative *to* Sinai (Exod. 15:22–18:27) appears to be strategic since it raises a question in the mind of the reader: "Where is an expression of faith?" What we find instead is complaining, and plenty of it (Exod. 15:24; 16:2, 7–8; 17:3).

6. Though this passage specifically refers to believing in Moses, the larger context makes clear that Israel demonstrated faith in God by believing and obeying what Moses said about God (see Exod. 4:1, 9, 31; especially 14:31).

people may "believe." *Faith is what God expects from Israel as the proper response to their Sinai experience.*

We move forward in the story expecting to find Israel's faith. We are quite surprised to discover, however, the exact opposite: unbelief and death. In the next major narrative section, the Wilderness Narrative *from* Mount Sinai to the Promised Land (Num. 10:11–36:13), the people of Israel do not believe: "And the LORD said to Moses, 'How long will this people despise me? And how long will they not believe in me, in spite of all the signs that I have done among them?'" (Num. 14:11). Then we are shocked to learn that even Moses and Aaron are not granted access to the Promised Land because they do not believe: "And the LORD said to Moses and Aaron, 'Because you did not believe in me, to uphold me as holy in the eyes of the people of Israel, therefore you shall not bring this assembly into the land that I have given them'" (Num. 20:12).

Israel's lack of faith is so pivotal in the story line that Moses looks back on the experience and tells us twice in Deuteronomy (the final narrative section of the Torah) that Israel did not believe!

> Yet in spite of this word you did not believe the LORD your God. (Deut. 1:32)

> And when the LORD sent you from Kadesh-barnea, saying, "Go up and take possession of the land that I have given you," then you rebelled against the commandment of the LORD your God and did not believe him or obey his voice. (Deut. 9:23)

The Lord clearly desires a faith response from his people. He acts on their behalf so they will believe.

Remarkably, the words "faith" and "righteousness" are mentioned together only twice in the whole Torah. In Genesis 15, we find "faith" and, consequently, we find "righteousness" (Gen. 15:6). Sadly, in Deuteronomy 9, there is no faith (Deut. 9:23), and, consequently, no righteousness (Deut. 9:4–6).[7]

---

7. No wonder Paul quotes the first part of Deuteronomy 9:4 in Romans 10:6 ("do not say in your heart") when comparing the righteousness based on the Law

Let's stop and consider the implications of faith versus no faith in the Torah. Before the giving of the Law, there is faith. In Exodus 19:9, at the introduction of the Sinai Narrative, it is quite clear that faith is supposed to be Israel's response to God at Mount Sinai. Although we would expect Israel to respond to God in faith once they have received the Law at Mount Sinai (i.e., faith under the Law), no faith is forthcoming. In spite of Israel's year-long experiences with God at Mount Sinai, Israel does not believe. As a direct result, and in contrast to the believing Abraham, they also do not have righteousness (Deut. 9:4–6). Therefore, they are not permitted to enter into the Promised Land (Num. 14:11; 20:12; Deut. 1:32; 9:23).

Sinai: Before and After

What does Israel's reception of the Law produce, if not faith? It is only when we compare Israel's Wilderness Narrative *to* Mount Sinai (before giving of the Law) with Israel's Wilderness Narrative *from* Mount Sinai (under the Law) that we find the answer. Consider these two Wilderness Narratives, *before* and *after* the Law is given, as bookends surrounding the giving of the Law.

There are numerous parallels between Israel's journey through the wilderness *to* Mount Sinai and their journey through the wilderness *from* Mount Sinai to the Promised Land:[8]

1. Israel complains after a three-day journey (Exod. 15:22, 24; Num. 10:33; 11:1), and the complaining continues for the remainder of the journey (Exod. 15:24; 16:2, 7–8; 17:3; Num. 14:2, 27, 29, 36; 16:11; 17:5, 10).
2. Israel longs for the food of Egypt (Exod. 16:3; Num. 11:4–5).
3. God provides manna and quail (Exod. 16:4–26; Num. 11:6–35).

---

with the righteousness based on faith: "For Moses writes about the righteousness that is based on the law, that the person who does the commandments shall live by them. But the righteousness based on faith says, 'Do not say in your heart . . .'" (Rom. 10:5–6). By quoting Deuteronomy 9:4, Paul expects his reader to see that Israel's lack of righteousness under the Law is the result of their lack of faith!

8. John H. Sailhamer, *Meaning of the Pentateuch* (Downers Grove, IL: InterVarsity Press, 2009), 366.

4. The Sabbath command is violated (Exod. 16:27; Num. 15:32).
5. Israel quarrels with Moses and asks why he brought them out of Egypt (Exod. 17:2–3; Num. 20:3–5, 13).
6. Israel questions the God who is among them (Exod. 17:7; Num. 11:20).
7. Israel's complaining occasions God's provision of water from the rock (Exod. 17:6; Num. 20:10–11).
8. Israel battles against the Amalekites (Exod. 17:8–16; Num. 14:43–45).
9. The people of Israel become so burdensome for Moses that he must appoint leaders to help him bear the load (Exod. 18:18–22; Num. 11:14, 16).

While Israel behaves in much the same way before and after the Law is given, the consequences of their actions are strikingly different:

1. Israel is victorious over the Amalekites before receiving the Law at Mount Sinai, but is defeated by them after Israel receives the Law (Exod. 17:13; Num. 14:43–45).
2. Moses does not complain about his burdensome dealings with the Israelites until Jethro points out the problem just prior to the giving of the Law on Mount Sinai (Exod. 18:18–22). As soon as he leaves Mount Sinai, however, when faced with the exact same problem, he asks God to kill him (Num. 11:14–15).
3. On their way *to* Mount Sinai, and just prior to the giving of the Law, none of the Israelites are put to death when they sin against God and/or against Moses. Many thousands, however, are put to death for the same offences once they receive the Law. For example:
   a. Violating the Sabbath goes unpunished in Exodus 16. Sabbath violators are put to death, however, after Israel receives the Law (Num. 15:36).
   b. Israel's longing for the delicacies of Egypt goes unpunished before the Law (Exod. 16). The Lord strikes down many Israelites with a plague for this same sin after they receive the Law (Num. 11:33; see also 14:37).

c. The people claim that it would have been better to die in Egypt before the Law (Exod. 16:2–3), but do not actually get their wish until the Law is given (Num. 14:2, 21–23, 32, 35).

d. Grumbling against Moses before the giving of the Law occasions no punishment (Exod. 16). After the Law is given, however, grumbling against Moses results in the death of about 15,000 people (Num. 16:1–3, 32–35; 16:41–42, 49). And yet again, when the people complain against the Lord and Moses, many are struck dead by fiery serpents (Num. 21:4–9).

Limitations of the Law

When we compare the before-the-Law picture of Israel with the under-the-Law picture of Israel, the implications are quite clear. Thus Paul expresses his understanding of the Torah in his New Testament writings when he articulates that the giving of the Law results in divine wrath and death, as in Romans 4:15: "For the law brings wrath, but where there is no law there is no transgression" (Rom. 5:20; see also Rom. 7:10; 2 Cor. 3:6). Moses' own perspective on the giving of the Law at Mount Sinai is perfectly consistent with Paul's understanding of the Law in his letters.

Moses is *not* presenting righteousness through the Law as Israel's key to blessing and the enjoyment of the Promised Land. As we have seen, he prophesies their disobedience to the Law, their exile, and the curses of the covenant both in the introduction and conclusion of the Torah. "I want to bless you with the gift of a very good land. By the way, you will be just like Adam. You will disobey the Law, experience curses, and die in exile. Here is the Law. I really hope you do better than I expect you will!"

Likewise, if Moses were presenting the Law as the key to Israel's righteousness, why would he highlight the vital connection between faith and righteousness before the Law, and then tell the story of Israel's breakdown of faith and lack of righteousness once God gave the Law? This would be akin to God saying, "I want to give you the same righteousness I gave Abraham when he believed, before I gave the Law. By the way, when I gave Israel the Law, they did not believe, and consequently I did not consider them righteous. Here is the Law. Good luck!"

Instead, the Torah story leads the reader to question the effectiveness of the Law for bringing Israel (and the nations) into the fullness of the unconditional promises of the Abrahamic covenant (see Gen. 15). Since the blessings of the Abrahamic covenant are unconditional, surely Israel's hope to receive them would not depend on obedience to the Law whose blessings are conditional, particularly because Moses makes it clear that future disobedience is certain.

We have carefully compared the behavior of the Israelites on their way *to* Mount Sinai, before receiving the Law, with their behavior on their way *from* Mount Sinai. Having spent an entire year with God at Mount Sinai,[9] having received the Law, the people's behavior does not change. They continue to complain and rebel against God and against his servant Moses. It is in this context that the exasperated Moses looks to a new source rather than the Law for the solution to Israel's problem: Moses looks to the giving of God's Spirit. "But Moses said to him [Joshua], 'Are you jealous for my sake? Would that all the LORD's people were prophets, that the LORD would put his Spirit on them'" (Num. 11:29). Moses does not say, "Would that all the LORD's people kept the Law." Moses' longing that all of Israel would receive God's Spirit is later picked up by the prophet Joel:

> And it shall come to pass afterward, that I will pour out my Spirit on *all flesh*; your sons and your daughters shall prophesy, your old men shall dream dreams, and your young men shall see visions. Even on the male and female servants in those days I will pour out my Spirit. (Joel 2:28–29 [Masoretic Text, 3:1–2], emphasis added)[10]

So far we have seen quite clearly that the Law cannot be the Torah's ultimate goal. If not the Law, then what—or *who*?

---

9. See Exodus 19:1; Numbers 10:11.

10. The Torah's story line clearly anticipates the importance of the giving of God's Spirit in Acts 2.

CHAPTER 3

The Torah's Remedy: The Messiah

We have looked at the story line of the Torah and argued that the introduction, conclusion, and body of the book do not support the commonly held belief that the Torah is a law book. Though the story line most certainly includes the giving of the Law, it also prophetically anticipates the breaking of that Law. It is one thing to speak about a prophetic anticipation. However, it is altogether another matter to suggest that the Messiah is the purpose of the Torah's story line, particularly when we take a moment to consider some percentages.

How many verses in the Torah refer to the Messiah and how many verses in the Torah refer to the Law? The percentages are staggering. There are about nine prominent verses in the Torah that people commonly consider messianic prophecies (Gen. 3:15; 49:8–12; Num. 24:17–19; Deut. 18:15), out of a total of 5,845 verses, or less than one fourth of one percent (0.15%). On the other hand, there are roughly 3,605 verses dealing with commandments given to the people of Israel.[1] This amounts to nearly 62% of all of the verses in the Torah. On percentages alone, we would have to say that the Law is far more important than the Messiah. The Law has to be the Torah's goal!

---

1. This figure is not intended to be exhaustive, but taken from a tally of all the verses in the following passages: Exodus 12 (the Passover), Exodus 16 (the Sabbath), Exodus 20–23, 25–31, 35–40; Leviticus 1:1–Deuteronomy 28:68.

Quantity Versus Quality

Before we come to hasty conclusions about the Torah's goal, let's consider an important principle in narrative literature: the principle of quality over quantity. For instance, if we were to ask who is the hero the C. S. Lewis's classic narrative *The Lion, the Witch, and the Wardrobe?*, without hesitation most people would say Aslan. Why is Aslan the hero of the narrative? He only shows up at the end of the book and most of the story line focuses on four children. Aslan is barely a blip on the screen when it comes to the percentage of time C. S. Lewis focuses on Peter, Edmund, Susan, and Lucy. How do we know Aslan is the hero? We can say that Aslan is the hero of the narrative because of the principle of quality, not quantity. Our equation does not depend on how much Aslan appears in the story, but where he appears in the story and how he brings the complications of the story's plot to resolution. Aslan not only shows up in qualitatively strategic places, but his character provides a resolution to the story line.

We believe the messianism of the Torah might likewise be considered in light of quality over quantity. Yes, the Law appears in 62% of the story, but as we have seen, the story line anticipates that Israel will break the Law and thereby break the Sinai covenant. A major obstacle in the Torah's plot is disobedience to God's Law and the consequences of the curses that come with disobedience (exile and death). We see this problem at the beginning and at the end of the Torah's story (Gen. 3; Deut. 28). Yet God's purpose for Israel and for all of humanity is blessing, another theme that appears at the beginning and end of the Torah (Gen. 1:28; Deut. 33). If disobedience to the Law is the obstacle for receiving God's blessing, what is the Torah's remedy?

The End Game

There are clues that the Torah's remedy, that is, the means through which God will accomplish his purposes to and through Israel, is the coming of the Messiah-King in the last days. Moses clearly regards "the last days" as a matter of great importance, since he uses the phrase four times in the Torah, and each is structurally significant. On three occasions, the phrase appears at the heading of very large prophetic poems: first, at the end of the Patriarchal Narratives (Gen. 49:1); second, when Balaam tries unsuccessfully to curse Israel at the transition period from the old to the new generation of Israelites in the wilderness (Num. 24:14); and third, at the end of the Torah as the prologue to the Song of Moses (Deut. 31:29).[2] The fourth time the phrase occurs is in the context of a prophecy, when Moses calls heaven and earth as witnesses (Deut. 31:28; 32:1) to the fact that Israel will be exiled from the land because of disobedience, but that in the midst of tribulation, Israel will return to the Lord in the last days (Deut. 4:25–31).

> Then Jacob called his sons and said, "Gather yourselves together, that I may tell you what shall happen to you in *the last days*." (Gen. 49:1)

> And now, behold, I am going to my people. Come, I will let you know what this people will do to your people in *the last days*. (Num. 24:14)

> When you are in tribulation, and all these things come upon you in *the last days*, you will return to the LORD your God and obey his voice. (Deut. 4:30)

> For I know that after my death you will surely act corruptly and turn aside from the way that I have commanded you. And in *the last days* evil will befall you. (Deut. 31:29)[3]

In each case, the phrase appears at such important junctions in the Torah story that, like the theme of faith, it must be considered a key for understanding the theological purposes of the Torah as a whole. Another clue to the importance of the last days is the opening word of the Torah itself: "In the beginning"—a word that in Hebrew requires an "end." The word in Hebrew for "last" in the phrase "the last days," is always used as the opposite of the word "beginning" in

---

2. Sailhamer, *Pentateuch as Narrative*, 35–37.

3. The ESV uses a translation other than "the last days" in each of the four verses. Because the phrase is exactly the same in the Hebrew in all four verses, we have changed the translation to "the last days," and have highlighted the change in italics. It is worth mentioning that our translation is a literal translation.

the Hebrew Bible (Num. 24:20; Deut. 11:12). The Torah opens with a story about the rise and fall of Adam in the "beginning of days." The Torah's introductory story serves as a prologue to God's ultimate plan to remedy mankind's greatest problem: our separation from God, caused by unbelief and disobedience. This remedy will not come *through* the Law, but *in spite of* Israel's repeated disobedience to the Law. Instead, God will provide the only sufficient remedy for sin through the Messiah-King in "the end of days" (see Gen. 49:1, 8–12; Num. 24:14, 17–19).

In what follows, we look at the importance of the Messiah within the story line of the Torah's narrative.

In the Beginning Was the Story

The fact that the Torah begins with narrative rather than commandments was, for the medieval rabbis, a problem in need of a solution. Rashi, the most famous of all Jewish Bible commentators, begins his commentary on the Torah by writing:

> Rabbi Isaac said, "The Torah should have begun with 'This month shall be for you' (Exod. 12:2), since this is the first commandment which Israel was commanded to keep." And what is the reason that it [the Torah] opens with 'In the beginning'?"[4]

Rashi goes on to explain that the Torah begins with a story, from creation to the exodus (Gen. 1–Exod. 12), in order to justify Israel's dispossession of the Canaanites from the Promised Land. Should the nations of the world accuse Israel of stealing the land from the seven Canaanite nations, Israel's defense would be THE STORY: "The whole world belongs to the Holy One blessed be He. He created it, and he gives it to whomever he sees fit." The story is Israel's "alibi": both her title deed to and justification for the conquest of the land.

Though the story may provide a divine justification for Israel's claim to the Promised Land, this is merely a subcategory of a far grander and universal purpose. It is our contention that the purpose

---

4. *Miqraot Gedoloth* (translation from Hebrew by the authors.)

of the story—a story that goes beyond Exodus to include the rest of the Torah as well as the Former Prophets (Joshua, Judges, 1–2 Samuel, 1–2 Kings)[5]—is to provide the biblical "alibi" for the messianic hope, as well as the eschatology in the Hebrew Bible as a whole.

Let's set the stage for this rather bold assertion with a few thoughts about the shaping and the nature of this story.

First, the Hebrew Bible, or Tanakh (the Law, the Prophets, and the Writings), opens with a single continuous historical narrative that starts with the creation of the world and concludes with the exaltation of Jehoiachin son of David in the Babylonian exile (2 Kings 25:27–30). This narrative accounts for nearly half of the entire Hebrew Bible in words.[6]

The Tanakh in Words

Torah	Prophets	Writings
Torah and Former Prophets (Genesis-2 Kings):	Latter Prophets and Writings (Isaiah-2 Chronicles):	
211,012 words	214,164 words	

---

5. For the purposes of clarity for those not familiar with the order of the Hebrew Bible, the order of the Hebrew Bible differs from the ordering of the Protestant Christian canon. The Hebrew canon is divided into three major sections based on the acronym "Tanakh," the Torah, the Prophets, and the Writings. The Prophets, moreover, are divided into the Former Prophets (Joshua-Kings), and the Latter Prophets (Isaiah-Malachi). One significant justification for using this tripartite arrangement in our study comes from Yeshua himself. Yeshua argues that the religious leaders would be held accountable for the blood of all the righteous martyrs from Abel (Gen. 4:8–16) to Zechariah (2 Chron. 24:21; see Matt. 23:35; Luke 11:51). Such a statement only makes sense when one thinks of the Hebrew Bible as beginning in the Torah and ending in Chronicles (i.e., Yeshua holds them accountable to the totality of revelation as expressed in the Hebrew Scriptures). Elsewhere, Yeshua provides the disciples with an exposition of the Messianic hope of the Scriptures, namely, Moses, the Prophets, and the Psalms (Luke 24:44). At the very least, we can say that Yeshua's presentation suggests he understood the Scriptures in terms of three sections, though we might be further inclined to argue that Yeshua not only viewed the Hebrew Bible in terms of three sections, but that he conceived the third section in terms of Psalms-Chronicles. In that case, the term "Psalms" in Luke 24:44 may have been used as a title for the entire third section of the Hebrew Scriptures.

6. Stephen G. Dempster, *Dominion and Dynasty* (Downers Grove, IL: InterVarsity Press, 2003), 39.

Second, the conclusion of this story can be anticipated by the reader since its plot is already foreshadowed in the introduction (Gen. 1–11). In rabbinic literature this phenomenon falls under the category of *ma'asei avot, siman l'banim* as discussed before, meaning "the deeds of the fathers are a sign to the sons."[7] In other words, the early chapters of this story, particularly the story of what becomes of Adam and Eve, are there not simply to tell us about what happened to Adam in the past but to tell what *will happen* to Israel in the future. Adam's story in Genesis 1–3 becomes Israel's story in the books of Joshua all the way through to 1–2 Kings (the gift of the garden/the land, the receiving of the commandments, the failure to resist the temptations of the resident(s) of the garden/the land, disobedience, and exile to the east).

Third, the prophetic nature of the Torah's introduction is reinforced by Moses' predictions at the end of the Torah:

> And the LORD said to Moses, "Behold, you are about to lie down with your fathers. Then this people will rise and whore after the foreign gods among them in the land that they are entering, and they will forsake me and break my covenant that I have made with them. Then my anger will be kindled against them in that day, and I will forsake them and hide my face from them, and they will be devoured. And many evils and troubles will come upon them, so that they will say in that day, 'Have not these evils come upon us because our God is not among us?' And I will surely hide my face in that day because of all the evil that they have done, because they have turned to other gods. Now therefore write this song and teach it to the people of Israel. Put it in their mouths, that this song may be a witness for me against the people of

---

7. See *Gen.Rab.* 48.7; Ramban's Commentary on Genesis 12:6. For example, Abram's sojourn in Egypt, which includes a famine in the land, the taking of Sarai into Pharaoh's service, the plagues on Pharaoh's house, Abram's departure with abundant gold, silver, and cattle, are clearly a "sign" to his sons, who likewise begin their sojourn in Egypt because of a famine, are taken into Pharaoh's service, set free through plagues, and depart with abundant gold, silver, and cattle. Abram's exodus from Egypt serves to foreshadow Israel's exodus from Egypt.

Israel. For when I have brought them into the land flowing with milk and honey, which I swore to give to their fathers, and they have eaten and are full and grown fat, they will turn to other gods and serve them, and despise me and break my covenant. And when many evils and troubles have come upon them, this song shall confront them as a witness (for it will live unforgotten in the mouths of their offspring). For I know what they are inclined to do even today, before I have brought them into the land that I swore to give." (Deut. 31:16–21)

Moses, the greatest of all the prophets of the Hebrew Bible, declares in no uncertain terms that Israel, like their father Adam, will enter the land, eat of its fruit, break God's commandments as expressed in the Sinai covenant, and be driven into exile (see Deut. 4:25–28; 30:1).

When we consider these three points—the substantial narrative of Israel's disobedience and subsequent exile, the foreshadowing of a story theme in Adam's disobedience and subsequent exile, and Moses' explicit predictions of Israel's disobedience and subsequent exile—a question forces itself upon us: Since Israel's disobedience and exile are anticipated and predicted by Moses in the Torah, what's the point of the story? Since Moses knew beforehand that Israel will break the Sinai covenant and go into exile, and that is precisely what happened in the Former Prophets, then the primary goal of the story is not to encourage Israel's obedience. What is the ultimate goal of the Torah, and the entire Hebrew Bible for that matter, if Israel's disobedience and exile are assured? We believe that the best answer to that question may be summed up in one word: "messianism." The Messiah, as we will see, is the point of the story, and the Messiah in the Torah story becomes the "buzz" of Israel's later sacred writings (the Latter Prophets and the Writings).

What Is Messianism?

According to some Bible scholars, messianism is a rather marginal topic in the Hebrew Bible.[8] The seemingly limited number of overt

---

8. See, for example, Gordon D. Fee and Douglas Stuart, *How to Read the Bible for All It's Worth* (Grand Rapids: Zondervan, 2003), 182; Grant R. Osborne, *The*

messianic prophecies in the Hebrew Bible, particularly in the Torah, may cause intellectual dissonance with clear statements in the New Testament about the centrality of the Messiah in the Tanakh. For instance, Yeshua makes the following rather bold claim about the Torah: "Do not think that I will accuse you to the Father. There is one who accuses you: Moses, on whom you have set your hope. For if you believed Moses, you would believe me; for he wrote of me. But if you do not believe his writings, how will you believe my words?" (John 5:45–47). Other statements in the New Testament claim unreservedly that the Messiah is *a* central, if not *the* central theme of Moses and the Prophets.[9] As followers of Yeshua who accept the authority and veracity of the New Testament, we honor Yeshua's claims about the Torah, though some might be hard-pressed to defend them from the *bema* (the pulpit) with just the Torah in hand. We would claim that messianism is a major theme in the Torah, and more, that it provides the headwaters out of which messianism flows to the rest of the Hebrew Bible.

Let's define the terms "messianism" and "Messiah" given the fact that these terms are not used in the Torah—and very infrequently in the Hebrew Bible for that matter—to describe the one about whom this chapter is written. The word "messiah" (*mashiach*, "anointed one") is used 39 times in the Tanakh, and on some occasions, though rarely, is used as a technical term to refer to the one whom later post-biblical writers call "the Messiah-King" (see, e.g., Ps. 2:2; Dan. 9:25–26).[10] In its non-technical sense, the term refers to the high priest (Lev. 4:3), to kings (1 Sam. 24:6), to prophets (Ps. 105:15), and to Cyrus (Isa. 45:1). Here we use "Messiah" as an all-inclusive term for the individual through whom God will ultimately reestablish his

---

Hermeneutical Spiral, revised ed. (Downers Grove, IL: InterVarsity Press, 2006), 264–65. In Osborne's words, "Fee and Stuart argue that less than 2 percent of the Old Testament prophecy is messianic, less than 5 percent relates to the new covenant age and less than 1 percent concerns events still future to us. . . . Of course, this figure depends largely on exegetical decisions as to which so-called messianic prophecies were originally intended messianically. Nevertheless, the percentage either way would be relatively low."

9. See, for example, Luke 24:25–27, 44; John 1:45; Acts 3:18; 24:14; 26:22, 27; 28:23; Rev. 19:10.

10. See Michael Rydelnik, *The Messianic Hope* (Nashville: B&H, 2010), 2.

original purposes for creation in the last days. At times, this multi-faceted figure is depicted as a king, other times as a prophet, and in some places as a priest. In some passages, he is described as a potentate, in others, a despised and rejected worm. In all cases, however, he is the lynchpin of God's plan to reestablish his blessed rule over a temporarily curse-ridden creation. "Messiah" refers to the hero of this story, and "messianism" is the term used to highlight those features that are pertinent to His-Story.

The Creation Mandate

If we seek to read the Torah according to its literary genre, we would be wise to search for the key themes of the story line in its opening chapters, given the fact that opening chapters in biblical literature, the Tanakh and New Testament alike, frequently introduce the key themes and ideas of the books as a whole. As we shall see, Genesis 1:26–28 introduces the major themes that are developed in the remainder of the Torah:

> Then God said, "Let us make man in our image, after our likeness. And let them have dominion over the fish of the sea and over the birds of the heavens and over the livestock and over all the earth and over every creeping thing that creeps on the earth." So God created man in his own image, in the image of God he created him; male and female he created them. And God blessed them. And God said to them, "Be fruitful and multiply and fill the earth and subdue it, and have dominion over the fish of the sea and over the birds of the heavens and over every living thing that moves on the earth." (Gen. 1:26–28)

The typical pattern of the creation week is as follows: "And God said" + "Let there be" + "And there was morning, and there was evening, an X day." However, there are two instances in the creation account that break one or more of these features of predictable literary patterns of Genesis 1:1–2:3.

First, the pattern is broken with the creation of humankind on the sixth day, as, instead of "Let there be" God uses words of divine deliberation: "Let us make." Second, the seventh day lacks both divine speech and an end. These disruptions of the pattern are intentional, drawing our attention to themes that will play an important role as the Torah's story continues to unfold. The broken pattern from "Let there be" to "Let us make"[1] on the sixth day draws the reader's attention to the theme of human rule over the land and everything in it, a prominent feature of what is called *the creation mandate.*

God's Threefold Promise

The creation mandate includes the three themes of Genesis 1:28 that make up the promises contained in the Abrahamic covenant. These three themes form the basis of God's dealings with and purposes for the people of Israel, namely, blessing, seed, and dominion over the land:

> And God blessed [*blessing*] them. And God said to them, "Be fruitful and multiply [*seed*] and fill the earth and subdue it [*land*],[2] and have dominion over the fish of the sea and over

---

1. Although Rashi argues that God is speaking with the angels, the fact remains that angels are nowhere referenced in the first chapter of Genesis. God and the Spirit of God (Gen. 1:1–2) are, however, present in Genesis 1. Properly speaking, God is not alone in the creation account. Support for the unity and plurality of God ("Let us make . . . in our image") is found when we notice verse 27. There we find a unity and plurality in man: "in the image of God he created him; male and female he created them." Man (singular), properly speaking, is represented by male and female (plural), a unity in plurality. Remarkably, this same feature is reflected grammatically in the reference to the plurality of the One True God in Genesis 1:1–2. The verb used to describe God in Genesis 1:1 is grammatically masculine: "In the beginning, God created [masculine singular verb] the heavens and the earth." The verb used to describe the Spirit of God in Genesis 1:2 is feminine: "And the Spirit of God was hovering [feminine singular verb] over the face of the waters." We are not arguing that God is ontologically both a male and a female. Rather, we are arguing that the unity in plurality of the One Creator is described with both masculine and feminine verbs, and this unity and plurality is reflected in the creation of humankind in the image of God.

2. True to the emphasis on the number seven in the creation account, "the land" is mentioned seven times in the creation mandate (Gen. 1:26–30).

the birds of the heavens and over every living thing that moves on the earth." (Gen. 1:28)

Two aspects of the creation mandate are directly tied to the Abrahamic covenant, which are generally masked by the English translations. First, the man and woman are called to exercise dominion over the *eretz*, a word that may be translated as "earth" or "land," depending on the context. When *eretz* is translated as "earth," one easily misses the fact that the creation mandate includes one of the three major components of God's threefold promise to Abraham, and to Israel, the gift of the *eretz* (land). Second, the creation mandate specifically includes a command to *kavash* the *eretz*. The typical translation, "subdue the earth," blurs the rather obvious connection to another key component of the Abrahamic covenant, the conquest of the Promised Land (*kibbush ha'eretz*). Later on in the Torah and the Former Prophets, this phrase is used explicitly to refer to Israel's conquest of the Promised Land (Num. 32:22, 29; Josh. 18:1). What is more, this same verb is used of King David's conquest of the nations in 2 Samuel 8:11, following on the heels of the making of the Davidic covenant in 2 Samuel 7.

In short, blessing, seed, and land are the central themes of the story from Genesis through 2 Kings. These themes also form the foundation for biblical eschatology. God's purpose in creation and in the election of Israel is to bless, multiply, and establish his rule over the land through the seed of the woman (Gen. 3:15).

Adam: God's First King

Having considered the creation mandate as the primary plot of the story, let's see how these three themes converge in Adam and Eve. Their story anticipates Israel's story and points to God's creation purposes for humanity.

Adam—understood as humankind, male and female, made in the image of God—is a king. The terminology used to describe rule and dominion in the creation mandate is used elsewhere to describe the rule of kings, language that, "coincidentally," is also repeated in some well-known messianic prophecies. The Hebrew word *radah* is the first of several dominion terms used in the creation mandate.

"Then God said, 'Let us make man [*adam*] in our image, after our likeness. And let them have dominion [*radah*] over the fish of the sea and over the birds of the heavens and over the livestock and over all the earth and over every creeping thing that creeps on the earth'" (Gen. 1:26). This term is used to describe Solomon's rule over the land in 1 Kings 5:4 [4:24 English versions]. Remarkably, though not surprisingly, this verb also appears in three passages that are traditionally regarded as messianic:

And one from Jacob shall exercise dominion [*radah*] and destroy the survivors of cities!" (Num. 24:19)	May he have dominion [*radah*] from sea to sea, and from the River to the ends of the earth! (Ps. 72:8)*	The LORD sends forth from Zion your mighty scepter. Rule [*radah*] in the midst of your enemies! (Ps. 110:2)

God intends to establish his rule over creation through *Adam* and his seed.

Adam: God's First Priest

To appreciate Adam's priestly role, we must first recognize the extent to which creation-Eden imagery permeates the tabernacle. Scholars have long noted many thematic and verbal parallels between the creation week and the Tabernacle Narrative (Exod. 25–31, 35–40), some of which are worth noting here.[3]

1. As the creation week is divided into seven days (Gen. 1:5, 8, 13, 19, 23, 31; 2:1), so the blueprints of the tabernacle are given in seven speeches (Exod. 25:1; 30:11, 17, 22, 34; 31:1; 12), and in both cases, the seventh day and the seventh speech focus on

---

* See Zechariah 9:10b, another well-known messianic prophecy whose words are nearly identical with Psalm 72:8.

3. See, for example, Shimon Bakon, "Creation, Tabernacle and Sabbath," *Jewish Bible Quarterly* 25, no. 2 (April 1, 1997): 79–85; Michael A. Fishbane, *Biblical Text and Texture: A Literary Reading of Selected Texts* (Oxford: Oneworld, 1998), 12; Peter J. Kearney, "Creation and Liturgy: The P Redaction of Ex 25–40," *Zeitschrift für die alttestamentliche Wissenschaft* 89 (1977): 375–87; Morales, *Tabernacle Pre-Figured: Cosmic Mountain Ideology in Genesis and Exodus* (Louvain, Belgium: Peeters, 2012).

the Sabbath. In the former, the Sabbath is the climax of creation; in the latter, the Sabbath is the sign of the covenant.

2. The creation and the construction of the tabernacle conclude with statements of completion (Gen. 2:2; Exod. 40:33b).

3. Once creation/construction are completed, they are inspected (Gen. 1:31a; Exod. 39:43a).

4. The creation and tabernacle are blessed (Gen. 1:22, 28; 2:3; Exod. 39:43b).

5. "The Spirit" is vital to the creation/construction process (Gen. 1:2; Exod. 31:3; 35:31).

6. The Creation Narrative and the Tabernacle Narrative both include accounts of a "fall" (Gen. 3; Exod. 32). In addition to these literary parallels, both accounts include a high degree of terminology unique to these narratives.[4]

Parallels between Creation and the Tabernacle

Creation	Tabernacle
Statement of Completion	*Statement of Completion*
And on the seventh day God finished [*kalah*] his work [*malakah*] that he had done, and he rested on the seventh day from all his work that he had done. (Gen. 2:2)	So Moses finished [*kalah*] the work [*malakha*]. (Exod. 40:33b)

---

4. The word for "lights" in Genesis 1:14–16 is only used elsewhere in the Torah to describe the Menorah (Exod. 25:6; 27:20; 35:8, 14, 28; 39:37; Lev. 24:2; Num. 4:9, 16). The process of separation, so vital to creation (e.g., light from darkness, water from water, night and day), is also vital to the priestly legislation (Gen. 1:4, 6–7, 14, 18; Exod. 26:33; Lev. 1:17; 5:8; 10:10; 11:47; 20:24–26; Num. 8:14; 16:9, 21). The specific form of the verb for "yield seed" in Genesis 1:11 is used elsewhere only in Leviticus 12:2. The distinction of the animals "according to their kind" in Genesis 1:6–7, is elsewhere only used with respect the classification of clean and unclean animals in the Torah (Gen. 1:11–12, 21, 24–25; 6:20; 7:14; Lev. 11:14–16, 19, 22, 29; Deut. 14:13–15, 18). The Hebrew root for the word "expanse" is only used elsewhere in the Torah with respect to the tabernacle and its service (Gen. 1:6–8, 14–15, 17, 20; Exod. 39:3; Num. 16:39). Finally, the focus on dietary provisions/restrictions in Genesis 1:29–30 is essential to the Mosaic Law (see Lev. 11; Deut. 14).

Inspection	Inspection
And God saw [v'yar] everything [et kol] that he had made, and behold [hinneh], it was very good. (Gen. 1:31a)	And Moses saw [v'yar] all the work [et kol], and behold [hinneh], they had done it; as the LORD had commanded, so had they done it. (Exod. 39:43a)
Benediction	Benediction
And God blessed them [v'yivarech otam]. (Gen. 1:22, 28; see 2:3)	Then Moses blessed them [v'yivarech otam]." (Exod. 39:43b)
Spirit of God	Spirit of God
And the Spirit of God was hovering over the face of the waters. (Gen. 1:2)	And I have filled him with the Spirit of God, with ability and intelligence, with knowledge and all craftsmanship (Exod. 31:3).

In addition to the many parallels between creation and the tabernacle, there are also numerous links between the garden of Eden and the tabernacle.[5]

1. We are told that God "walks" [hithalekh] in the midst of the garden. The form of this verb is also used to describe God's activity in the tabernacle (Gen. 3:8; Lev. 26:12; Deut. 23:14).
2. God stations cherubim on the eastern entrance to the garden, clearly parallel to the decorative cherubim whose presence on the veil guard the eastern entrance into the Holy of Holies (Gen. 3:24; Exod. 26:31; Num. 3:38).
3. The tree-like menorah in the sanctuary is likely intended to be a replica of the tree of life in the midst of the garden (Gen. 2:9; Exod. 25:32–36).
4. The precious metals that are mentioned in the garden of Eden Narrative are mentioned elsewhere in the Torah with

---

5. For the classic treatment of the links between the garden and the tabernacle, see Gordon J. Wenham, "Sanctuary Symbolism in the Garden of Eden Story," I Studied Inscriptions before the Flood, ed. Richard Hess and David Toshio Tsumura, Sources for Biblical and Theological Study 4 (Winona Lake, IN: Eisenbrauns, 1994), 399-404. The following list of parallels draws heavily upon Wenham's work.

reference to the precious metals used in the construction of the tabernacle (Gen. 2:12; Exod. 25:7; 28:9–14, 20; Num. 11:7).[6]

Once we recognize that Eden is portrayed as the prototypical creation-sanctuary, Adam's role as the prototypical priest over all creation comes to light. First, we are told that Adam is placed in the garden to *work* and to *watch* over it. This twofold commission over the garden is, in fact, the same twofold commission given to the Levites, namely, to *work* and *watch* over the tabernacle (Gen. 2:15; Num. 3:7–8).[7] Moreover, having sinned, God clothes [*hilbish*] Adam's nakedness with a tunic [*kutonit*], a phrase that is used most frequently in the Torah to describe the clothing of the priests in the tabernacle (Gen. 3:21; Exod. 29:8; 28:39–40), which, significantly, is intended to cover their nakedness (Exod. 28:40–43).

Adam is the prototypical high priest over all creation, and all subsequent divinely ordained high priesthoods trace their origins back to Adam in the garden. Aaron's annual task of passing beyond the images of the cherubim to the place where God walks with his people (Lev. 16:2) serves as a reminder of Adam's once privileged position in Eden before the Fall (see Gen. 3:8, 24). The connection between Adam's original priesthood and the Aaronic high priesthood is most notably highlighted by the prophet Ezekiel, who depicts the king of Tyre in the likeness of Adam in the garden before his fall, adorned with all the stones upon the high priestly garments:

You were in Eden, the garden of God; every precious stone was your covering, sardius, topaz, and diamond, beryl, onyx,

---

6. It is clear enough that the prophets, by describing the future temple in terms of a renewed Eden, also regard the garden of Eden as the prototypical temple of creation from which all other sanctuaries are patterned (compare, for instance, the river flowing out of Eden with the river flowing forth from the eschatological temple: Gen. 2:10–14; Ezek. 47).

7. Andrew J. Schmutzer, "The Creation Mandate to 'Be Fruitful and Multiply': A Crux of Thematic Repetition in Genesis 1–11," (PhD diss., Trinity Evangelical Divinity School, 2005), 348. He writes, "Just as Eden is God's garden-sanctuary, the prototypical temple, so the terms 'keeping and guarding' . . . are used for priests who 'serve' God in the temple and 'guard' it from all unclean things."

and jasper, sapphire, emerald, and carbuncle; and crafted in gold were your settings and your engravings. On the day that you were created they were prepared. You were an anointed guardian cherub. I placed you; you were on the holy mountain of God; in the midst of the stones of fire you walked. You were blameless in your ways from the day you were created, till unrighteousness was found in you. (Ezek. 28:13–15)[8]

Ezekiel's allusions to Eden are unmistakable. Significant for our purposes is the list of gemstones used to describe Adam's covering. These are the very stones that are used to adorn Israel's high priest (Exod. 28:17–20; see also Rev. 21:19–20).

What are we to make of the parallels between the Creation Narrative and the construction of the tabernacle, and between the garden of Eden and the design of the tabernacle itself? In a recent publication, Michael Morales looks at the lexical and thematic parallels between Genesis 1–3 and Israel's story in Exodus: from the parted seas (of creation/of the exodus) to the tabernacle of his presence (Eden/tabernacle).[9] Morales highlights the parallels between the Creation Narrative and the construction of the tabernacle (Gen. 1:1–2:3; Exod. 25–31, 35–40), and between the priestly ministry of Adam in Eden and the priestly ministry of Aaron in the tabernacle (Gen. 2:4–3:24; Exodus-Numbers). He argues convincingly that the land in Genesis 1:1–2:3 is depicted as the outer courtyard to a cosmic temple, with the garden of Eden serving at its Holy of Holies (Gen. 2:4–9).[10] The effect of this depiction is clear: God places Adam in the garden-sanctuary as the high priest par excellence, the high priest in the garden and king over all creation. Adam's royal-priestly depiction clearly anticipates God's call on Israel collectively to be a royal

8. Though this passage has typically been understood as a reference to the fall of Satan, the depiction of this high priestly figure in Eden is more likely an allusion to Adam, given the fact that Genesis 2–3 portrays Adam, and not the serpent, as a priest. C. F. Keil and Delitzsch F., "Ezekiel, Daniel," *Commentary on the Old Testament*, vol. 9 (Peabody, MA: Hendrickson, 1996), 410, write, "Ezekiel here compares the situation of the prince of Tyre with that of the first man in Paradise; and then, in verses 15 and 16, draws a comparison between his fall and the fall of Adam."

9. Morales, *Tabernacle Pre-Figured*, 51–120.

10. Ibid., 90.

priesthood (Exod. 19:6), and God's call on Aaron individually to be the one who serves the God who walks with his people beyond the cherubim.

Now we are ready to consider the royal-priestly Adam as a prefiguration and sign of things to come (i.e., the deeds of the fathers are a sign to the sons), both in terms of *collective* Israel as well as an *individual* who will arise from Israel's midst. What happens when Adam is not able to live up to the creation mandate, and what does that say about Israel's future? Does Adam's/Israel's failure nullify God's purposes of blessing through his creation mandate?

CHAPTER 5

The Adam-Israel Connection

Israel's disobedience, according to the prophet Hosea, is in the likeness of Adam's disobedience. "But like Adam they transgressed the covenant; there they dealt faithlessly with me" (Hosea 6:7). Positively, *adam* (male and female) is blessed for the purpose of filling the *eretz* (land) and conquering it (Gen. 1:28). The description of Israel's phenomenal growth in the land of Egypt draws a direct link to the creation mandate: "But the people of Israel were fruitful and increased greatly; they multiplied and grew exceedingly strong, so that the land was filled with them" (Exod. 1:7). It is clear enough that this growth can be none other than a result of God's promised *blessing* of Abraham's seed (cf. Exod. 1:9; Gen. 18:18; Num. 22:6). It is in Egypt that God takes a small family and turns them into a people, he creates them to be a nation outside the land, just has he created Adam outside the garden, ultimately to be brought into it. In fact, the term used for bringing or placing Adam in the garden is specifically used in Deuteronomy and Joshua to describe God's action of bringing Israel into the Promised Land (Gen. 2:15; Deut. 12:10; Josh. 22:4).[1]

It is likely not a coincidence that the term used for subduing in the creation mandate is later used to describe King David's subjugation of the nations (Gen. 1:28; 2 Sam. 8:11); and the terms for ruling over creation and its animals are used to describe King Solomon's rule (1 Kings 5:1, 4, 13 [English versions 4:21, 24, 33]). Adam's mandate, and

---

1. The geographical location of the garden, like the Promised Land, is marked by the rivers surrounding it (Gen. 2:10–14; 15:18).

subsequently Israel's, is accomplished vicariously through Israel's reigning king (as can also be seen in Ps. 8:5–9 [English version 8:4–8]).

Adam's continued habitation of the garden is contingent upon obedience to God's commandments. Obedience means life in the garden; disobedience means death in exile (Gen. 2:16–17; 3:19, 23–24). Likewise, under the Sinai covenant Israel's habitation of the Promised Land is contingent upon obedience to God's commandments. Obedience means life in the land; disobedience means death in exile (Deut. 30:15–20).[2]

Clever and Cursed

Once Adam is brought into the land, however, the mandate to conquer the land and rule over its inhabitants, and the commandment to choose life rather than death, are thwarted by an inhabitant of the garden who is described as more *clever* (*arum*) than the other creatures of creation (Gen. 3:1). Adam and Eve quickly succumb to the tempter's enticements. The serpent's rebellion results in its being cursed (Gen. 3:14). Likewise, Israel's initially successful military campaign to conquer the land and its inhabitants is quickly undermined by very *clever*, yet subsequently cursed inhabitants.

Now the serpent was more crafty [clever; *arum*] than any other beast of the field that the LORD God had made. . . . The LORD God said to the serpent, "Because you have done this, cursed are you above all livestock and above all beasts of the field; on your belly you shall go, and dust you shall eat all the days of your life." (Gen. 3:1, 14)	But when the inhabitants of Gibeon heard what Joshua had done to Jericho and to Ai, they on their part acted with cunning [*beormah*] and went and made ready provisions and took worn-out sacks for their donkeys, and wineskins, worn-out and torn and mended. . . . "Now therefore you are cursed, and some of you shall never be anything but servants, cutters of wood and drawers of water for the house of my God." (Josh. 9:3–4, 23)

---

2. The terminology used to describe Israel's choices and the consequences of disobedience in Deuteronomy 30:15–20 is an intentional allusion to Adam's choices and the consequences of disobedience in Genesis 2–3: life and death, good and evil, blessing and curse.

The result of Joshua's covenant with these native inhabitants is the descent into apostasy as Israel is enticed by their gods, and subsequent exile from the Promised Land comes as punishment.[3] Thus Joshua, like Moses before him, can say with assurance that Israel will break the covenant by serving other gods, given the ongoing presence of the Canaanites in the land (Josh. 23:15–16; Deut. 31:16–21). Given these clear predictions in the Torah and in Joshua, we are not surprised to read in Judges about the terrible dangers awaiting Israel because of the continued presence of the Canaanites:

> Now the angel of the LORD went up from Gilgal to Bochim. And he said, "I brought you up from Egypt and brought you into the land that I swore to give to your fathers. I said, 'I will never break my covenant with you, and you shall make no covenant with the inhabitants of this land; you shall break down their altars.' But you have not obeyed my voice. What is this you have done? So now I say, I will not drive them out before you, but they shall become thorns in your sides, and their gods shall be a snare to you." (Judg. 2:1–3)

By the Rivers of Babylon

Returning to the story of Adam and Eve, we read that their disobedience results in their being cast out of the garden—eastward—where they eventually die in exile (Gen. 3:23–24; 5:5). Adam's children continue their easterly exilic movement away from the special garden-land until they eventually find themselves in Babylon (Gen. 11:1–9). It is out of Babylon that God brings forth an individual seed—a descendent of Adam and Eve, of Seth, of Noah, and of Shem—back to the garden-land in order to conquer it, to rule over it and to reestablish the blessing that was so tragically lost through Adam's fall

---

3. The numerous references to the commands of Deuteronomy 7:1–4 (not to make a covenant with the Canaanites lest they tempt Israel to follow other gods) in Joshua 9 (see vv. 15, 24), strongly suggest that the author sees Joshua's covenant with the Gibeonites as the beginning of the end of Israel's successful campaign to conquer the Promised Land—and more importantly, to fulfill the creation mandate in Adam's stead (see Deut. 11:16).

(Gen. 11:10–12:9). In short, God chose Abram to restore his blessed rule over creation through the seed of the woman.

Israel's story in the Former Prophets follows along these predictable lines. Though God chooses an individual dynasty of kings through whom Israel will ultimately fulfill Adam's calling (the dynasty of David), its fulfillment is not to be realized before Israel's foreseen covenant disobedience and subsequent exile—to Babylon of all places (2 Kings 25; see Deut. 4:26–30). Here we see that the concluding verses of the Former Prophets serve as the sign to which the deeds of the fathers *(ma'asei avot)* in Genesis 1–11 point. Just as Adam's disobedience brings him and his descendants to Babylon (Gen. 11:1–9), so Israel's disobedience brings her and her descendants to Babylon (2 Kings 25). What is more, just as the tale of the "first Babylonian exile" in Genesis 11 concludes on a hopeful focus on an individual seed (Abraham) through whom God will reestablish his creation purposes, likewise the telling of the "second Babylonian exile" concludes with a hopeful focus on an individual seed (Jehoiachin) through whom God will ultimately reestablish his creation purposes (compare Gen. 12:1–3 and 2 Kings 25:27–30).

The Torah's Poems

So then it is entirely predictable that Israel will collectively fail to fulfill the creation mandate under the Sinai covenant and will be punished for disobedience with exile. Again, following the pattern, it is only to be expected that Israel's ultimate fulfillment of the creation mandate will come through a king from the tribe of Judah. In his groundbreaking work on the Deuteronomic history (Deuteronomy–2 Kings), Martin Noth points out one of the key literary devices by which the biblical author interprets Israel's story, namely, through large speeches or poems.[4] John Sailhamer, likewise, highlights the significance of large speeches in the Torah's narrative,

---

4. Martin Noth, *The Deuteronomistic History* (Sheffield: Sheffield Academic Press, 1981), 5. By saying that the speeches are a literary device, we are by no means denying the historicity of these speeches. Rather, we are suggesting that the location of these speeches in key moments in Israel's history as told in the Former Prophets and the common repeated themes contained therein strongly suggest that these speeches not only bring connectivity to Israel's history but also sense and meaning.

speeches that are poetic in genre and appear at major junctions of the Torah story.[5]

Poetic Speeches in the Torah Story
God's Response to the Fall (Gen. 3:14–19)
Jacob Blesses His Sons (Gen. 49)
The Song of Moses (Exod. 15)
The Oracles of Balaam (Num. 23–24)
The Song of Moses and Moses' Final Blessing on Israel
(Deut. 32–33)[6]

The common language and repeated themes shared by most if not all the poetic speeches in the Torah suggest that these poems do in fact provide both literary and theological cohesiveness to the Torah story as a whole. Significantly, three of the four largest poetic speeches found in the Torah are identified as events that will take place in the last days (Gen. 49:1; Num. 24:14; Deut. 31:29).[7]

In the next three chapters we will discuss the following three poetic speeches and their significance, not only for understanding the theology of the Torah but also in terms of the messianism of the Hebrew Bible:

God's Response to the Fall (Gen. 3:14–19)
Jacob Blesses His Sons (Gen. 49:1–28)
The Oracles of Balaam (Num. 24:1–24)

---

5. John Sailhamer, *Pentateuch as Narrative* (Grand Rapids: Zondervan, 1995), 36.

6. Other poetic speeches not included in this list are the following: Genesis 2:23; 9:25–27; 12:1–3; 24:60; 27:28–29; Exodus 17:16; Numbers 21:17–18, 27–30.

7. The fourth poem is found in Exodus 15:1–21 and is known as the Song at the Sea.

CHAPTER 6

Poem One: God's Response to the Fall (Genesis 3:14–19)

In order to appreciate Genesis 3 in general and Genesis 3:14–19 in particular, let's recall that Adam, who is portrayed as God's son,[1] is mandated by God to conquer the land and to rule over all its creatures. Given the fact that the Torah story begins with "the beginning" of days, Adam's story tells of humanity's first "king"—the king whose rule begins in *the beginning of days*, who is tempted by the serpent, and who thereby fails to conquer the land and rule over it. He forfeits this divinely ordained rule over the land, is cast into exile, and by virtue of his banishment from the garden-sanctuary, loses his priesthood. It is only from the frame of reference of Adam's royal-priestly calling over creation that God's calling to Israel at Mount Sinai makes sense: "And you shall be to me a *kingdom* of *priests* and a holy nation" (Exod. 19:6, emphasis added). In Genesis 3:14–19, God not only pronounces judgment upon the serpent, the woman, and the man but also lays out (in intentionally ambiguous terms).[2] His

---

1. God, by virtue of his place at the head of the list of Adam's genealogies, implicitly portrays Adam as the son of God through whom God intends to rule over creation (see Gen. 5:1–4). If Adam is Seth's father, and Seth is Enosh's father, who is Adam's father? The answer is clearly—God!

2. John Sailhamer, *Genesis*, Expositor's Bible Comentary, vol. 2 (Grand Rapids: Zondervan, 1990), 56, commenting on Genesis 3:15, writes, "Verse 15 still contains a puzzling yet important ambiguity: Who is the 'seed' of the woman? It seems obvious that the purpose of this verse has not been to answer that question but rather to raise it. The remainder of the book is the author's answer."

plan to restore the kingship and the priesthood to humanity. God intends to reestablish his dominion over creation through the seed of the woman!

> The LORD God said to the serpent, "Because you have done this, cursed are you above all livestock and above all beasts of the field; on your belly you shall go, and dust you shall eat all the days of your life. I will put enmity between you and the woman, and between your offspring and her offspring; he shall bruise your head, and you shall bruise his heel." (Gen. 3:14–15)

In our attempts to understand this text in terms of messianism, let us first answer three important questions:

1. Is the serpent just a reptile?
2. Is the seed of the woman a reference to a collective entity (Israel) or an individual (the Messiah)?
3. Who receives the more deadly blow—the seed of the woman or the serpent?

Garden-Variety Reptile?

Although the Torah, or the whole Hebrew Bible for that matter, never explicitly identifies the serpent as the devil,[3] the text clearly portrays the serpent as unique among all his other created beings (with the exception of humans of course). The serpent is more clever than all other beasts of the field, the evidence of which is demonstrated in its ability to talk, reason, and even oppose God's word. Moreover, though it's clear enough from the text that the serpent's rebellion results in ongoing battles between the serpent's seed and the woman's seed, the war will not come to an end until the serpent itself is dealt with. In other words, the text suggests that the serpent outlives its seed. The New Testament writers are quite justified in identifying the serpent as humanity's archenemy, the devil.

---

3. The New Testament, however, does identify the serpent as the devil (Rev. 12:9; 20:2; Rom. 16:20 is very likely an allusion to Gen. 3:15).

The Seed of the Woman:
Collective Israel or Individual Messiah?

In order to interpret this text, it is crucial to note that the use of the word "seed" is intentionally ambiguous. In the Hebrew language, "seed" can be interpreted as a collective (descendants), but it can also be interpreted as an individual (descendant). Genesis 3:15 forces a strategically important question upon its readers, the answer to which can be found by carefully reading the rest of the Torah story.

Is the seed who will crush the serpent's head a collective group of people (Israel), or is it an individual? To answer this question, let's consider this passage syntactically and contextually. Jack Collins, in his careful study on the syntactical distinctions between the collective and individual use of the term seed,[4] concludes that pronouns are crucial in determining whether seed is collective or singular. Whenever seed refers to a collective entity, the pronouns referring to it are always plural. For instance, we read in Genesis 15:13: "Then the LORD said to Abram, 'Know for certain that your *offspring* [seed] will be sojourners in a land that is not *theirs* [plural pronoun] and will be servants there, and *they* [plural pronoun] will be afflicted for four hundred years'" (emphasis added). [5]

When seed, according to Collins, refers to an individual, its pronouns are always singular: "And I will make a nation of the son of the slave woman also, because *he* [singular pronoun] is your *offspring* [seed]" (Gen. 21:13, emphasis added).[6] Here seed clearly refers to Ishmael, and thus the singular pronoun "he" is used. Such is the case in Genesis 3:15 as well: "And I will put enmity between you and the woman, and between your seed and her *seed*; *he* [singular pronoun] shall bruise you on the head, and you shall bruise *him* [singular pronoun] on the heel" (emphasis added).

Though Collins's syntactical conclusions have been generally accepted, they are not entirely conclusive. Particularly problematic to his theory is Genesis 22:17–18: "I will surely bless you, and I will

---

4. Jack Collins, "A Syntactical Note (Genesis 3:15): Is the Woman's Seed Singular or Plural," *Tyndale Bulletin* 48.1 (1997), 139–49.

5. Other examples of the word "seed" used with plural pronouns include Genesis 17:7–10; 48:11–12.

6. Other examples include 1 Samuel 1:11; 2 Samuel 7:12–15.

surely multiply your *offspring* [seed] as the stars of heaven and as the sand that is on the seashore. And your *offspring* [seed] shall possess the gate of *his* [singular pronoun] enemies, and in your *offspring* [seed] shall all the nations of the earth be blessed, because you have obeyed my voice" (emphasis added). Here the word seed is used three times, the first of which is unambiguously plural: "*offspring* [seed] as the stars of heaven." The second time seed appears, however, it is used with a singular pronoun: "And your *offspring* [seed] shall possess the gate of *his* [singular] enemies." We are faced with an interpretive challenge. Does the first instance of seed, which is clearly collective, determine the meaning of the second pronoun, "the gate of *their* [singular pronoun with a collective meaning] enemies"? Or can we interpret the second and third instances in these verses to refer to a single individual through whom the nations will find blessing?

Thankfully, there is evidence elsewhere in the Hebrew Bible that helps us in interpreting this verse. Psalm 72 is a structurally significant Psalm in the Psalter, serving as a conclusion to Books I and II of the Psalter.[7] Psalm 72 shares significant parallels with Psalm 2, a psalm that is formally recognized by many scholars, along with Psalm 1, as the introduction to Book I. Psalm 2 and 72 focus on an exalted Davidic king whose rule extends to the ends of the earth (Pss. 2:8; 72:8). What is more, Psalm 72 contains several allusions to some of the Torah's poetic speeches,[8] suggesting that its author looked to this Messiah-King as one through whom the Torah's key prophecies would find fulfillment. Helpfully, Psalm 72:9 and 17 offer an inner-biblical interpretation of Genesis 22:17–18 with respect to the identity of the seed:

May desert tribes bow down before him, and his enemies lick the dust! . . . May his name endure forever. May his name endure forever, his fame continue as long as the sun!	I will surely bless you, and I will surely multiply your offspring as the stars of heaven and as the sand that is on the seashore. And your offspring shall possess the gate of

7. Book I (Pss. 1–41), Book II (Pss. 42–72).

8. Compare Psalm 72:8 with Numbers 24:19 and Zechariah 9:10–11; Psalm 72:9 with Genesis 3:14; and Psalm 72:11 with Genesis 27:29.

May people be blessed in him, all nations call him blessed! (Ps. 72:9, 17)	his enemies, and in your offspring [seed] shall all the nations of the earth be blessed. (Gen. 22:17–18)

It is quite clear that Psalm 72:17 is a nearly verbatim allusion to Genesis 22:18, and as such the psalmist looks at "*his* enemies" in the prior verse as referring to an individual seed of Abraham, and thus interprets the seed through whom all the nations will be blessed in Genesis 22:18 as an individual king. This is our first clue that the seed of the woman is an individual: "*he* shall bruise your head."

Who or what is the serpent's seed? Several clues in the story line of the Torah suggest that the serpent's seed does not refer to baby snakes, but rather to opponents of the chosen seed of the woman. For example, in the very next chapter we read of Cain, who finds himself cursed after opposing Abel (cf. Gen. 4:11; 3:14). Likewise, Ham's perverted actions result in his son's sharing of the serpent's fate as well: "Cursed be Canaan" (Gen. 9:25). Later on in Genesis 12:3, we are told that all who curse Abraham (and his seed) will also share the serpent's fate: "And him who dishonors you I will curse." According to the Torah's story line, therefore, the serpent's seed are those who curse the chosen seed, and thus share the serpent's fate.

In Genesis 4, the chapter that immediately follows the prophetic promise in Genesis 3:14–15, Adam's firstborn kills Abel, and in response God gives Eve another seed. Remarkably, Eve's commentary on God's provision uses terminology in Genesis 3:15 only found elsewhere in the entire Hebrew Bible:

And Adam knew his *wife* [woman] again, and she bore a son and called his name Seth, for she said, "God *has appointed* for me another offspring [*seed*] instead of Abel, for Cain killed him." (Gen. 4:25, emphasis added)*	*I will put* enmity between you and the *woman,* and between your offspring [seed] and her offspring [*seed*]; he shall bruise your head, and you shall bruise his heel. (Gen. 3:15)

---

* Italics in the following parallel passages are added to show comparison.

The word "wife" in Genesis 4:25 is the same word for "woman" in Genesis 3:15. Moreover, Eve's statement "God has appointed" uses the same verb for "put" in Genesis 3:15: "I will *put* enmity." Finally, Eve states that God has appointed for her another "seed." Eve's allusions to Genesis 3:15 in Genesis 4:25 are quite clear in the Hebrew text. And it is equally clear that Eve has interpreted the reference to "her seed" in Genesis 3:15 not in its collective sense, but as speaking of an individual son who will defeat the serpent.

Who Receives the Worse Blow—the Seed or the Serpent?

For many people, the answer to this question is so clear that the question itself is not worth asking. Truth be told, however, the question is a trap. The answer to the question is not either/or but both/and. Some might protest: "Wait a minute; a blow to the head is far more severe than a blow to the foot." That might be true enough if we are speaking of man versus man. But we are not. This is man versus serpent. When a man wants to kill a serpent, of course he strikes its head. But when a serpent wants to kill a man, it bites the foot, the truth of which is made abundantly clear in Genesis 49:17: "Dan shall be a serpent in the way, a viper by the path, that bites the horse's heels so that his rider falls backward." Strangely enough, God's judgment against the serpent includes a prediction that the seed of the woman shall also suffer a fatal blow. Does this mean, however, that the Torah story ends in tragedy—nobody wins, everyone loses? Or does this mean that ultimate victory over the serpent will be achieved but at great expense? As we look at the two other poetic speeches regarding the last days in the Torah, Genesis 49 and Numbers 24, we will see that the Torah story has a happy ending. However, Genesis 3:15 not only prepares the reader for predictions of the glories of the coming Messiah-King but also paves the way for appreciating the sufferings of the coming Messiah-King. God's purposes in Genesis 1:28 will come to fruition, but the reclamation of creation includes great suffering and death.

One Seed of the Woman: Noah

We see that in a very real sense, Genesis 3:15 is the fountainhead of messianism. Though Adam has abdicated both his kingship and priesthood over creation, and though collective Israel will be like

Adam, Genesis 3:15 anticipates the coming of an individual seed of woman, a priest-king, another Adam, who will ultimately defeat the serpent and his descendants, though not without a terrible struggle. In order to complete our appreciation of the meaning of Genesis 3:15, let us briefly consider the story of Noah, another Adam and king-priest, who is called to reestablish God's creation purposes.

That the Torah's author sees the seed of the woman as a future Adam-like figure is evident in his presentation of Noah. This is most evident in the occasion by which Noah ("rest" in Hebrew) is given his name. "And called his name Noah [rest], saying, 'Out of the ground that the LORD has cursed, this one shall bring us relief from our work and from the painful toil of our hands'" (Gen. 5:29).[9] Clear allusions to the poetic speech of Genesis 3:14–19, particularly to Genesis 3:17–19, suggest that Noah is portrayed as a seed of the woman who will, at least in a limited sense, restore the creation to its pre-fall conditions. How will Noah, Mr. Rest, bring rest to creation? We will have occasion to answer that question in a moment. But for now we must stop and ponder the figure Noah as the answer to the Torah author's expectations for the fulfillment of Genesis 3:15. The seed of the woman will be another Adam who will reverse Adam's failures.

In terms of "the deeds of the father are a sign for the sons" (*ma'asei avot*), we should expect to find many clear parallels between Noah and Adam, both in terms of their victories, and sadly enough, in terms of their downfalls. First, we see that like Adam before him, God also brings the animals to Noah as a demonstration of his dominion over

And God blessed Noah and his sons and said to them, "Be fruitful and multiply and fill the earth. The fear of you and the dread of you shall be upon every beast of the earth and upon every bird of the heavens, upon everything that creeps on the ground and all the	And God blessed them. And God said to them, "Be fruitful and multiply and fill the earth and subdue it, and have dominion over the fish of the sea and over the birds of the heavens and over every living thing that moves on the earth." And God said, "Behold, I have given you

---

9. The Hebrew word for "relief" shares two of the same Hebrew consonants with the word "rest," and is clearly used as an intentional word play on Noah's name.

creation (Gen. 2:19; 7:9; cf. 1:28). Second, once God brings Noah and his children safely through his judgment, Noah receives a slightly revised form of the creation mandate and blessing.

fish of the sea. Into your hand they are delivered. Every moving thing that lives shall be food for you. And as I gave you the green plants, I give you everything. But you shall not eat flesh with its life, that is, its blood." (Gen. 9:1–4)

every plant yielding seed that is on the face of all the earth, and every tree with seed in its fruit. You shall have them for food. And to every beast of the earth and to every bird of the heavens and to everything that creeps on the earth, everything that has the breath of life, I have given every green plant for food." And it was so. (Gen. 1:28–30)

Noah, like his father Adam, is blessed (*blessing*), commanded to fill the land (*seed*), and is given authority over the creatures of creation (*land*). And in both cases, the mandates are followed by dietary provisions as well as dietary restrictions.

Not only is Noah like Adam in his dominion over the animals and in his creation mandate, but third, he is like him in his downfall. Note the similarities between the Adam Fall Narrative and the Noah Fall Narrative: the planting of a garden/vineyard (Gen. 2:8; 9:20), the taking of its fruit (Gen. 3:6; 9:21), shameful nakedness (Gen. 3:7; 9:21), the knowing of something shameful (Gen. 3:7; 9:24) the covering up of nakedness (Gen. 3:7, 21; 9:23), and the pronouncing of a curse involving subjugation (Gen. 3:14; 9:25). Sadly, Noah's fall shows that he is *a* seed of the woman, but not *the* seed of the woman. His victory is partial, but not final, and thus the war between the seed of the woman and the seed of the serpent, in this case the Canaanites (Gen. 9:25), will continue.

But now we must ask ourselves: In what sense did Noah bring rest from the curse of Genesis 3? By building an ark? By surviving the flood? No! Noah's greatest achievement, in terms of the story, was not the building of the ark and the surviving of the flood, but the fulfilling of a priestly role—by building an altar and offering a sacrifice! This is most clearly marked by the poetic use of Noah's name, or forms of it, throughout the story. Noah (*noach*) will bring comfort (*nacham*) to the land (Gen. 5:29). God regrets (*nacham*) that he made man, but Noah (*noach*) finds favor (*chen* = *noach* spelled backwards) in God's eyes (Gen. 6:6–8). The ark rests (*nuach*) upon the mountain in the seventh month (Gen. 8:4), but the dove does not find a resting place (*manoach*) for its foot (Gen. 8:9). The climax of the narrative, however, is reached when Noah builds an altar, sacrifices offerings to the Lord (Gen. 8:20), the aroma from which is *pleasing* (*nichoah* = from the same root as Noah's name) to the Lord (Gen. 8:21). It is only at this point in the story that Noah's actions do justice to the meaning of his name: "to give rest (comfort) from the curse." And so we read in Genesis 8:21:

> And when the LORD smelled the pleasing [restful] aroma, the LORD said in his heart, "I will never again curse the ground because of man, for the intention of man's heart is evil from his youth. Neither will I ever again strike down every living creature as I have done."

There is one beyond Noah, a seed of the woman, the new Adam of Genesis 3:15, who will reestablish God's purposes for creation, not merely by reigning as a king but also by functioning as a priest. The priest offers sacrifices to restore peace and rest. The New Adam (the singular seed) will enjoy the glories of victory (crushing the head) as well as having to pay the sacrifice of suffering and death (being struck in the heel) to reclaim what was lost in Genesis 3. All kingship and priesthood in the Tanakh ultimately finds its origins in one figurehead: Adam. And all messianism in the Hebrew Bible, be it royal or priestly, also finds its source in Adam.

Poem Two: Jacob Blesses His Sons (Genesis 49:1–28)

The importance of the coming seed of the woman, a New Adam, is most apparent in the genealogies of Genesis. Very quickly the lines are divided, as the author of the Torah blazes a genealogical trail from Adam through Shem (Gen. 9:26–27) to Abraham (Gen. 12:1-3) to Isaac (Gen. 22:17-18) to Jacob (Gen. 27:28-29), all the while separating the chosen from the not-chosen seed in order to find Adam's truest descendent. Oddly, the story of Judah and Tamar is rather abruptly inserted into an otherwise seamless narrative about Jacob's beloved son Joseph (Gen. 38).[1] The point of this pause in the main narrative, both in terms of the genealogical concerns in Genesis and of the Davidic line, is to move from Adam through Judah to Perez (Gen. 38:29; see Ruth 4:18).[2] Subtle clues in Perez's birth narrative, in fact, depict Perez as another Jacob, thereby making him the heir through whom the fullness of God's promises to Jacob in Genesis 25:23 and 27:28-29 will come:

---

1. Gordon J. Wenham, *Genesis 16–50*, Word Biblical Commentary (Waco, TX: Word, 1987) 363, writes, "At first blush, chap. 38 seems to have nothing to do with the Joseph story. If it were omitted, the narrative would progress from 37:36 to 39:1 very smoothly. It does not appear to be necessary for understanding chaps. 39–50."

2. Ruth is of vital importance in connecting the messianism of the Torah to the House of David. David is not only of the tribe of Judah, he is also a descendant of Perez.

When the time of her labor came, there were *twins in her womb*. And when she was in labor, one put out a hand, and the midwife took and tied a *scarlet thread* on his hand, saying, "This one came out first." But as he drew back his hand, behold, his brother came out. And she said, "What a breach you have made for yourself!" Therefore his name was called Perez. *Afterward his brother came out with the scarlet thread on his hand*, and his name was called Zerah. (Gen. 38:27–30)

When her days to give birth were completed, behold, there were *twins in her womb*. The first came out *red*, all his body like a hairy cloak, so they called his name Esau. *Afterward his brother came out with his hand holding Esau's heel, so his name was called Jacob*. Isaac was sixty years old when she bore them. (Gen. 25:24–26)

The birth narratives of Perez and Jacob are remarkably similar. Both tell of twins who struggle in their mother's womb. In both cases, the younger supplants the older brother, the former by grabbing his brother's heel, the latter by pushing his brother aside. And in both narratives, the displaced brother is identified by the color red, the former by his hair, the latter by the scarlet thread attached to his hand.

Three Sons Step Aside

Having highlighted this important, yet frequently overlooked parallel between Jacob and Perez, we are now ready to consider the significance of Genesis 49 for the messianism of the Hebrew Bible and of the Torah in particular. To recall, Jacob's poetic blessing is explicitly identified as a prophecy about the last days in Genesis 49:1: "Then Jacob called his sons and said, 'Gather yourselves together, that I may tell you what shall happen to you in [the last days].'" Though identified as a blessing in Genesis 49:28, Jacob's words about Reuben, Simeon, and Levi in Genesis 49:2–7 do not, at first glance, appear to be a blessing. Reuben is called out for sleeping with Bilhah (Gen. 35:22). Simeon and Levi are destined to be scattered in Israel because of their cruel deception and violent actions to the men of Shechem (Gen. 34:25–30). Jacob's harsh words to Reuben and Levi just prior to his death and burial contrast so starkly with Moses' words of blessing to Reuben (see Deut. 33:6) and Levi (see Deut. 33:8–11) just prior to his death and burial that it begs the question: Why is Jacob so harsh to the first three of his twelve sons?[3] The answer to this question has to do with the purpose of Jacob's blessing in the larger context of Genesis. Genesis's consistent focus on tracing the chosen line has led us from Adam through the seed of woman to Abraham (Gen. 6:9; 11:10, 27) to Isaac (Gen. 25:19) and to Jacob (Gen. 37:2). And though all of Jacob's twelve sons are the chosen people (Gen. 49:28; Exod. 1:1–5; Deut. 33:1, 29), the story line drives us on to a single seed, the New Adam, who will rule over the nations and defeat the serpent and its seed. Thus, it's not that Jacob is casting aside his first three sons from the people of Israel, but rather that they are stepping aside to make way for the King through whom they will also be blessed!

> Judah, your brothers shall praise you; your hand shall be on the neck of your enemies; your father's sons shall bow down before you. Judah is a lion's cub; from the prey, my son, you have gone up. He stooped down; he crouched as a lion and as a lioness; who dares rouse him? The scepter shall not depart from Judah, nor the ruler's staff from between his feet, until tribute comes to him; and to him shall be the obedience of the peoples. Binding his foal to the vine and his donkey's colt to the choice vine, he has washed his garments in wine and his vesture in the blood of grapes. His eyes are darker than wine, and his teeth whiter than milk. (Gen. 49:8–12)

Jacob's blessing of Judah has been traditionally, and correctly, interpreted as a messianic prophecy that the Messiah-King would come from the tribe of Judah.[4] But for our purposes, we must not overlook the ways in which Jacob's prediction of the king of the last days fits within the larger story line. First, it is crucial to notice that Judah's role as a tribe in the plan of God is to receive his brothers' allegiance:

---

3. Simeon does not appear in the Blessing of Moses.

4. See, for example, Targum Onkelos; M. Sanhedrin 98.72; Genesis Rabba 98.8; Midrash Bereishit 97.13; Rashi; Ramban.

"your brothers shall praise you . . . your father's sons shall bow down before you" (v. 8). Jacob's words concerning Judah—"*your father's sons shall bow down before you*"—are practically identical to Isaac's words to Jacob: "Let peoples serve you, and nations bow down to you. Be lord over your brothers, *and may your mother's sons bow down to you.* Cursed be everyone who curses you, and blessed be everyone who blesses you!" (Gen. 27:29, emphasis added).

What is most striking about Isaac's oracle concerning Jacob, "be lord over your brothers. . . . May your mother's sons bow down to you," is the extent to which the Jacob-Esau story contradicts the promise! First, Jacob only has a single brother, thus "your brothers" and "your mother's sons" simply do not fit. Second, though Jacob is called to be the master of his brothers, in the story of Jacob and Esau's reunion, Jacob consistently refers to himself as "your servant" and Esau as "my lord" (Gen. 32:4–5, 10, 18, 20; 33:5, 8, 13–15). Third, though Isaac prophecies concerning Jacob that "your mother's sons bow down to you," we are explicitly told that Jacob and his family are the ones that bow down to Esau (Gen. 33:3, 6–7). Why does the author go to such great lengths to show that Jacob's relationship with Esau doesn't line up with Isaac's prediction? The answer, it would appear, is that Isaac's words, though spoken to Jacob, will ultimately be fulfilled through Jacob's seed, whom Jacob later identifies as the king from the tribe of Judah (Gen. 49:8). It is through this king that the blessings and/or the curses of the Abrahamic covenant will come: "Cursed be everyone who curses you, and blessed be everyone who blesses you" (Gen. 27:29b; see Num. 24:9b).

Birthright Blessings

A later biblical author notices and comments on the promises to Jacob in Genesis 27:29 and its connection with the tribe of Judah in Genesis 49:8. In 1 Chronicles 5:1–2 we read:

> The sons of Reuben the firstborn of Israel (for he was the firstborn, but because he defiled his father's couch, his birthright was given to the sons of Joseph the son of Israel, so that he could not be enrolled as the oldest son; though Judah

became strong among his brothers and a chief came from him, yet the birthright belonged to Joseph).

The Chronicler's phraseology betrays his biblical sources. His comments concerning Reuben are taken from Genesis 49:3–4. The reference to the birthright blessings being given to Joseph are taken from Genesis 48:1–22; 49:22–26. What of the comment "though Judah became strong among his brothers and a chief came from him"? Remarkably, the Hebrew form of this phrase is found in only one other place in the Hebrew Bible: Genesis 27:29 ("Be lord over your brothers"). By alluding to Genesis 27:29, the writer of Chronicles makes Isaac's blessing of Jacob and Jacob's prediction concerning Judah explicit: peoples will serve Jacob, the nations will bow down to Jacob, Jacob will be lord over his brothers, and blessings will come to Israel and the nations (see Gen. 27:29) through Jacob's greatest descendent.

Returning to the reference to the father's sons bowing down to Judah (Gen. 49:8), one is also immediately struck by the similarity to the story of Joseph. In fact, the whole point of the Joseph Narrative is to tell the story of how Joseph's eleven brothers will bow down to him as the divinely chosen ruler (Gen. 37:7–10; 42:6; 43:26, 28; 48:12), much to their chagrin and in spite of their opposition. What is the point, therefore, of telling the Joseph story if God's purposes for world redemption will ultimately come through Judah? *Ma'asei avot, siman l'banim*: the deeds of the fathers are a sign for the sons. Joseph's story is intended to be an illustrative prophecy/story of future events. The story of Joseph's rise to power by rejection, suffering, and ultimate triumph is the dramatized version of Jacob's poetic oracle in Genesis 49:8–12.

There are important details in Genesis 49:8–12 that serve to bind Jacob's prediction into the larger story line. For instance, this king of the last days will grab his enemies by the back of the neck (v. 8), or in other words, by the head! Moreover, the obedience of the nations will be his (v. 10; see Gen. 27:29). Triumph over enemies and dominion over the nations is a consistent and oft-repeated theme in the promises to Abraham, Isaac, and Jacob (see Gen. 22:17; 24:60; Num. 24:18), and can only be fully appreciated in light of Adam's original creation mandate and the predictions of Genesis 3:15. The seed of the woman, from the tribe of Judah, a king in the last days, will be the one to take the serpent and his seed by the neck! He will be the one who will reestablish Adam's mandate.

CHAPTER 8

Poem Three: Balaam's Oracles (Numbers 24:1–24)

Just as Jacob's poetic speech predicted the coming of the Messiah-King in the last days, likewise Balaam's oracles speak of the same king and the last days, and as we shall see, the two poems share important similarities. Before we look at Numbers 24, let us consider the Balaam Narrative in the larger context of the Torah's messianic story line, and not merely as random fragments of disconnected prophecies.

Balaam: Good Guy or Bad Guy?

What are we to make of Balaam in Numbers 22–24? Whose side is he on? On the one hand, he is presented as a Spirit-filled prophet who refuses to compromise the word of God (Num. 22:18; 24:2). On the other hand, he is depicted as a pagan diviner (Num. 24:1; Josh. 13:22) with less spiritual insight than a donkey (Num. 22:34).[1] What is more, he is eventually put to death by the sword because of his involvement with Israel's prostitution at Peor (Num. 31:8, 16). Before we look at what Balaam says about the Messiah, we must first figure out whether we should listen to him at all. After all, how can we trust the words of a pagan diviner who speaks from both sides of his mouth?

---

1. His brutishness is even reflected in his name, Balaam son of Beor, his father's name apparently a pun on the Hebrew word for fool (see Prov. 30:2).

Some rather obvious parallels between the stories of Balaam and his donkey (Num. 22:22–35) and Balak and Balaam (Num. 22:36–24:25) show us that we not only can but must believe the message in spite of the messenger. In the account of Balaam and his donkey, the spiritually blind Balaam unwittingly tries to force his spiritually insightful donkey to circumvent the Messenger of the Lord three times (Num. 22:28, 32, 33). Likewise, in the account of Balak and Balaam, the spiritually blind Balak tries to force the spiritually insightful Balaam to curse Israel three times (Num. 23:7; 23:27; 24:10). In both accounts, Balaam's third attempt (to force his donkey/to curse Israel) culminates in a divinely enabled "opening of the eyes" to behold things he had not seen before (Num. 22:31; 24:4, 15, 17).

Then the LORD opened the eyes of Balaam, and he saw the angel of the LORD standing in the way, with his drawn sword in his hand. And he bowed down and fell on his face. (Num. 22:31)	The oracle of him who hears the words of God, who sees the vision of the Almighty, falling down with his eyes uncovered [opened]. (Num. 24:4)

These parallels provide the reader with a frame of reference for evaluating Balaam's oracles in light of his personal character. The blind and perilous Balaam unwittingly fighting against the Messenger of the Lord in chapter 22 anticipates the blind and perilous Balak unwittingly fighting against God in chapters 23–24. Likewise, the perceptive donkey refusing to circumvent the Angel of the Lord in chapter 22 anticipates the perceptive Balaam refusing to curse Israel in chapters 23–24. These parallels encourage us to accept the message regardless of the messenger. How can such a dubious person speak forth such spiritually significant oracles? In the same way that a typically brutish beast is supernaturally enabled to see the Messenger of the Lord and to speak forth the truth. If God can speak through a donkey he can do the same through a pagan prophet. And if, like Balaam in chapter 22 and Balak in chapters 23–24, we fail to heed the words of the donkey and the words of the prophet, we do so at our own peril.

To Bless or To Curse?

In order to fully appreciate Balaam's poetic speeches, let's read them in the context of the larger story of the restoration of God's creation purposes through the seed of the woman, through Abraham and his descendant. Allusions to and citations of other key texts in the Torah make it clear that the focus of Numbers 22–24 is the outworking of the promised blessings and curses of the Abrahamic covenant, the culmination of which is the reign of Messiah-King in the last days (Num. 24:14, 17–19). Balak's statement to Balaam that "he whom you bless is blessed, and he whom you curse is cursed" (Num. 22:6; see v. 12; 24:9) draws directly from God's promises to bless those who bless Abraham and his seed and to curse those who curse Abraham and his seed (see Gen. 12:3; 27:29).[2] Noteworthy are the numerous references to the verbs "bless"[3] and "curse"[4] throughout this section, the highlight of which is when Balaam learns the unchangeable truth that it is pleasing in the Lord's eyes to bless Israel (Num. 24:1). Moreover, the implicitly royal connotations of the Abrahamic covenant as expressed in Genesis 27:29 (see below) and later amplified in Genesis 49:8–12 are, as in Jacob's prophecy, explicitly tied to Israel's king in Numbers 24.

Let peoples serve you, and nations bow down to you. Be lord over your brothers, and may your mother's sons bow down to you. Cursed be everyone who curses you, and blessed be everyone who blesses you! (Gen. 27:29)	Judah, your brothers shall praise you; your hand shall be on the neck of your enemies; your father's sons shall bow down before you. (Gen. 49:8)	He crouched, he lay down like a lion and like a lioness; who will rouse him up? Blessed are those who bless you, and cursed are those who curse you. (Num. 24:9)

---

2. Clearly related to the blessings and curses of the Abrahamic covenant is the promise of numerous descendants, the fact of which causes Balak to fear and to call for reinforcements (Num. 22:3–6; cf. Exod. 1:12). The theme of abundant descendants is central to the Torah's theology (compare Exod. 1:7, 9, 10, 12 with Gen. 1:28; 9:7; 17:2; 18:18; 22:17; 26:4, 24; 28:3; 35:11; 47:27; 48:4).

3. Numbers 22:6, 12; 23:11, 20, 25; 24:1, 9, 10.

4. Numbers 22:6, 11, 12, 17; 23:7, 8, 11, 13, 25, 27; 24:9, 10.

How does Balaam's Narrative tie the blessings and curses of the Abrahamic covenant specifically to the Messiah?

I See Him, but Not Now!

Numerical patterns are quite common in Scripture. In the case of the Balaam Narrative three's a charm. Earlier we looked at the parallels between Balaam and his donkey and Balak and Balaam. In both stories, the third attempt to fight against God's will results in the opening of Balaam's eyes to behold individuals of supernatural significance. Several textual clues in the narrative suggest that the author is intent on directing the reader's attention to the "third attempt" (to curse Israel) oracles in Numbers 24:

First, we are told that Balaam does not use enchantments as he had with the previous oracles (Num. 24:1).

Second, the narrator states that Balaam is empowered by the Spirit of God, a phenomenon attributed to only two other individuals in the Torah (compare Num. 24:2 with Gen. 41:38 [Joseph] and Exod. 31:3; 35:31 [Bezalel]).

Third, we are told that, unlike the other oracles where Balaam sees only a portion of the people of Israel, he sees all of Israel encamped tribe by tribe (Num. 24:2; see 22:41; 23:13).

Fourth, we are told that Balaam utters these oracles with "open eyes" (Num. 24:3–4, 15).

Fifth, the "third attempt" oracles are identified in Numbers 24 as prophetic utterances (*neum*) six times: vv. 3 (twice), 4, 15 (twice), 16; this term is used elsewhere in the Torah only two times (Gen. 22:16; Num. 14:28).

Why does the author go to such great lengths to draw attention to Balaam's third oracle? It seems the purpose is to emphasize the content of the vision Balaam receives when his eyes are supernaturally opened. In chapter 22, Balaam is supernaturally enabled to see the Messenger of the Lord. In chapter 24, Balaam's eyes are opened to see things that will take place in the "latter days," namely, the coming of the Messiah, the one through whom Adam's dominion over creation will once again be established; the one who will defeat the enemy by crushing his head (see Gen. 3:15); the one who will dispossess his enemies (see Gen. 22:17; 24:60).

And now, behold, I am going to my people. Come, I will let you know what this people will do to your people in the latter days [the last days]. . . . I see him, but not now; I behold him, but not near: a star shall come out of Jacob, and a scepter shall rise out of Israel; it shall crush the forehead of Moab and break down all the sons of Sheth. Edom shall be dispossessed; Seir also, his enemies, shall be dispossessed. Israel is doing valiantly. And one from Jacob shall exercise dominion and destroy the survivors of cities! (Num. 24:14, 17–19)

From "Them" to "Him"

Though the famous Jewish Bible commentator Rashi limits the messianism of Balaam's prophecy to Numbers 24:19, evidence suggests that all of Balaam's "third-attempt" oracles (Num. 24:7–9, 17–24) are messianic. First, note that Balaam's "third-attempt" oracles (including Num. 24:7–9) are remarkably similar to Judah's blessing in Genesis 49. Both places describe a royal figure (a lion, a scepter) who will come in the last days.

Judah is a lion's cub; from the prey, my son, you have gone up. He stooped down; *he crouched as a lion and as a lioness; who dares rouse him?* The *scepter* shall not depart from Judah, nor the ruler's staff from between his feet, until tribute comes to him. (Gen. 49:9–10)	*He crouched, he lay down like a lion and like a lioness; who will rouse him up?* Blessed are those who bless you, and cursed are those who curse you. . . . I see him, but not now; I behold him, but not near: a star shall come out of Jacob, and a *scepter* shall rise out of Israel. (Num. 24:9a, 17a)

These similarities strongly suggest that these passages refer to the same individual, namely, the Messiah.

Second, though some may argue against a messianic interpretation of Numbers 24:8–9 since the wording of the text is so similar to Numbers 23:22, 24, a passage clearly referring to Israel as a whole, the grammatical, syntactical, and contextual differences between these two passages suggest that Numbers 24:8–9 is not merely a repetition of Numbers 23:22, 24. Look at the difference:

God brings *them* out of Egypt and is for them like the horns of the wild ox. (Num. 23:22)

God brings *him* out of Egypt and is for him like the horns of the wild ox. (Num. 24:8a)

You will notice a difference in the pronouns used in Numbers 23:22: "them," and in 24:8: "him." Are these merely stylistic differences or do they serve a strategic purpose? To answer the question let's take a look at the immediate context in which these verses are found.

He has not beheld misfortune in *Jacob*, nor has he seen trouble in *Israel*. The LORD their God is with *them*, and the shout of a *king* is among them. *God brings them out of Egypt* and is for them like the horns of the wild ox. For there is no enchantment against Jacob, no divination against Israel; now it shall be said of Jacob and Israel, "What has God wrought!" Behold, a *people! As a lioness it rises up and as a lion it lifts itself, it does not lie down* until it has devoured the prey and drunk the blood of the slain. (Num. 23:21–24)

How lovely are your tents, O *Jacob*, your encampments, O *Israel*! Like palm groves that stretch afar, like gardens beside a river, like aloes that the LORD has planted, like cedar trees beside the waters. Water shall flow from his buckets, and his seed shall be in many waters; his *king* shall be higher than Agag, and his kingdom shall be exalted. *God brings him out of Egypt* and is for him like the horns of the wild ox; he shall eat up the nations, his adversaries, and shall break their bones in pieces and pierce them through with his arrows. *He crouched, he lay down like a lion and like a lioness; who will rouse him up?* Blessed are those who bless you, and cursed are those who curse you. (Num. 24:5–9)

When we take a closer look at Numbers 23:21–22 we notice that verse 21 refers to a king who is among the people of Israel, most likely the Lord in this context.[5] Notice that "Jacob" and "Israel," like "king," are all singular nouns, yet "Jacob" and "Israel" refer collectively to the whole people (they/them), whereas "king" (he/him) does not. In

---

5. See Philip J. Budd, *Numbers*, Word Biblical Commentary (Waco, TX: Word, 1984), 268; R. Dennis Cole, *Numbers*, New American Commentary (Nashville: Broadman & Holman, 2000), 413.

order to make it clear to the reader that Balaam is referring to Israel-Jacob and not to the king in the following verse, the author must use a plural pronoun ("them"), even though the plural pronoun does not agree in number with the singular "Israel/Jacob": "God brings *them* [Israel] out of Egypt." This is obviously a reference to Israel's exodus from Egypt.

Turning our attention to Numbers 24:7–8, we see that 24:7, like 23:21, also refers to Israel's king. "His [Israel's] king shall be higher than Agag, and his [the king's] kingdom shall be exalted." In this case, the king no longer refers to the Lord but to a future king who will arise out of the people of Israel.[6] When we look at the continuation of Balaam's oracle in 24:8, we can now appreciate the significance in the shift of pronouns: "God brings *him* out of Egypt." Why the shift? In Numbers 23:22, the author uses to the plural pronoun "them" in order to make it abundantly clear that he is referring to Israel's historical exodus from Egypt. By using the singular pronoun in Numbers 24:8, the author wants to make it just as clear that he is no longer referring to Israel and to her past; rather, he is referring to Israel's future king, a king who will prevail over Israel's enemies, a king whose kingdom will be exalted (Num. 24:7). In Numbers 23:22, God *brought* Israel ("them") out of Egypt. In Numbers 24:8, however, God *will bring* Israel's king ("him") out of Egypt!

Why does this interpretation of Numbers 24:8 make more sense? There are three reasons. First, it is supported by the grammar and syntax of the verse itself. Second, the whole point of the "third-attempt" oracles (Num. 24) is to point to spiritual realities that Balaam was unable to see in the earlier oracles. He now sees reality through spiritually opened eyes (see Num. 24:3–4, 16–17). A repetition of the description of Israel's exodus in Numbers 24:8 is foreign to the overall flow of the text. Although Balaam uses words quite similar to Numbers 23:22 to describe what he sees in Numbers 24:8,

---

6. "A star shall come out of Jacob, a scepter shall rise out of Israel" (Num. 24:17) is in all likelihood intended to clarify and explain the rather enigmatic poetry in Numbers 24:7: "Water shall flow from his buckets, and his seed shall be in many waters." What does "water shall flow from his [Israel's] buckets" mean? Numbers 24:17 explains it: a king will come forth from the people of Israel (compare Num. 24:7, 17 in the LXX [Septuagint]).

the changes in wording point to a previously unseen spiritual reality. In the earlier instance he could only see Israel's exodus from Egypt as a past event, but later he discovers harbingers of the future king foreshadowed in Israel's exodus (i.e., the deeds of the fathers are a sign for the sons). *Just as God brought Israel out of Egypt, so God will bring Israel's Messiah out of Egypt.*

The third reason to consider that the first mention of collective Israel gives way to a later mention of an individual king is that the identification of the "him" in Numbers 24:8 with the coming Messiah and not Israel is confirmed in Numbers 24:9 ("He crouched, he lay down like a lion and like a lioness; who will rouse him up? Blessed are those who bless you, and cursed are those who curse you."), a nearly verbatim quotation of another messianic prophecy (Gen. 49:9): "Judah is a lion's cub; from the prey, my son, you have gone up. He stooped down; he crouched as a lion and as a lioness; who dares rouse him?" *It is through this king that the promises of blessing to the patriarchs and in the mandate to Adam will be fully realized: "Blessed are those who bless you, and cursed are those who curse you"* (Num. 24:9b; see Gen. 27:29b; Ps. 72:17).

Having examined the evidence as seen in these three poetic speeches that the Torah's purpose is to point to a king who is the seed of the woman from the tribe of Judah coming in the last days, we are still left wondering about the Law. How we are to understand the Sinai covenant with its complex system of commandments if the Law is not the goal of the Torah? Why are there are so many verses about the Law in the Torah? What purpose does the Law serve? Where does its value lie? How do we relate to it as inspired, authoritative Scripture?

CHAPTER 9

Functions of the Law

In Galatians 3, Paul argues that long before the Law was given, God planned to bless Israel and the nations through faith in the coming Messiah. He then goes on to explain that those who rely on the works of the Law are under a curse (Gal. 3:10-13). This leaves us with the following quandary: if the Law (which results in a curse) came 430 years after a promise of blessing (Gal. 3:17-18), why in the world did God give the Law? Paul anticipates this question when he asks, "Why then the Law?" (Gal. 3:19). Though Paul's answer is not an exhaustive treatise on the subject, he provides one of several answers to this very important question. We also ask ourselves as both Jewish and Gentile followers of the Messiah Yeshua today, "Why the Law, and what is our relationship to it?" We will look at this question from the understanding that the entire Torah continues to be authoritative Scripture for the believer—*all of it*, including the Law.

Scripture gives us several functions of the Law: tutor, shadow, theology, love, wisdom, and prosecuting attorney.

The Law as Tutor

We have already noted that Paul regards the Law as something that came hundreds of years after God's promise to Abraham. Paul defines what he means by Law in the context of his discussion; this definition is essential to the argument. Paul speaks about Scripture in Galatians 3:8 and goes on to quote Genesis 12:3. In Galatians 3:17, he says that the Law was added 430 years after the promises were made to Abraham. Since the promises Paul mentions in Galatians

3:8 are also part of the Torah (i.e., Gen. 12:3), the "Law" added 430 years later must refer to the laws of the Sinai covenant and not to the Torah as a whole.

When we fail to see the fact that Law here cannot refer to the Torah as a whole, we run into all sorts of big theological problems, one of which is to assume that since we are no longer under the Law (i.e., the Sinai covenant) we are no longer under the authority of the Torah as Scripture. Paul not only refers to the Torah (Gen. 12:3) as Scripture[1] but also uses the Torah to prove his theological point: namely, justification by faith through the Messiah is the heart of the Torah's theology, whereas the Law (the commandments of the Sinai covenant) was added to the promise for a provisional purpose. For Paul, the Law (including the Sinai covenant with its commandments) is part of a larger story called the Torah, whose whole purpose is to lead us to faith in the Messiah. As Scripture, every part of the Torah, including the Law, continues to serve that purpose (see Gal. 3:22). So when we speak about the Law, we are specifically referring to the Sinai covenant and its legal stipulations, that is, the rules and regulations in operation until the making of the new covenant (see Heb. 8:13).

According to Paul, the Law "was added because of transgressions, until the offspring should come to whom the promise had been made" (Gal. 3:19). The Law was put in place as our guardian or tutor until the Messiah came (Gal. 3:24); the implication is that we are no longer under the authority of the Law. Where did Paul get this idea? From the Torah, of course! It is interesting to see that the giving of the Law does not take place in one huge deposit of 613 laws. Rather, we see in the Torah story that Israel's relationship to God under the Sinai covenant is dynamic—when Israel sins, new laws are added.

Take for example the commandment about adding tassels to garments in Numbers 15:37–41. God does not give this commandment to the people of Israel when they are at Mount Sinai. Why not? Because Israel does not need it yet. Rather, this commandment is

---

1. "And the Scripture, foreseeing that God would justify the Gentiles by faith, preached the gospel beforehand to Abraham, saying, 'In you shall all the nations be blessed'" (Gal. 3:8).

given in response to the events of Numbers 13–14. Here we read that Israel is commanded to spy out (*tor* in Hebrew, a key word throughout the Spy Narrative) the land (Num. 13:2), but fear gets the better of them and the ten spies sway the crowd to unbelief (Num. 14:11). The judgment is swift, and that generation is condemned to death in the wilderness because of their unfaithfulness (Num. 14:33). God uses a very harsh word for "unfaithfulness" which actually means "whoredom," that is, sexual unfaithfulness (the Hebrew root of this word is *zanah*).

Having sentenced the Israelites to death in the wilderness, Numbers 15 takes a surprising turn: "The LORD spoke to Moses, saying, 'Speak to the people of Israel and say to them, "When you come into the land you are to inhabit, which I am giving you"'" (Num. 15:1–2). Immediately after God condemns the first generation to death in the wilderness, he begins to provide Israel with instructions for when they will come into the land (God is good!).

The final law in this series of new laws is the commandment to wear tassels. Why tassels? God explains the commandment using the unique words borrowed from the previous story about Israel's failure to take the land: "And it shall be a tassel for you to look at and remember all the commandments of the LORD, to do them, not to follow after [*tor* in Hebrew] your own heart and your own eyes, which you are inclined to whore after [*zanah*]" (Num. 15:39). By using these specific words, it is clear that the commandment to wear tassels is a response to Israel's transgression in the previous story. Why the tassels? To prevent you from doing what you just did at Kadesh-barnea. The obvious implication is this: Had Israel not sinned in the previous narrative, they would not need an external reminder not to sin again![2]

The commandment to wear tassels functions in much the same way as a curfew for a rebellious teenager. If the teenager were more

---

2. There are other examples of specific commandments being added because of Israel's transgression. One obvious example would be the appointment of the Levites as a response to the golden calf (Exod. 32:26–29). Who functioned as Levites up until this point? Most likely it was the firstborn males from all the tribes, as a fulfillment of Israel's calling to be a kingdom of priests (see Num. 3:12). The transgression brings with it specific restrictions that were not in place beforehand.

mature, he would not need a curfew. Obviously, a loving father seeks ways to keep his child in check. But when the child grows up to become a mature adult, the curfew (the tutor) is no longer necessary. That is precisely Paul's point in Galatians 3:19–29. It is also his point in 1 Timothy:

> Now we know that the law is good, if one uses it lawfully, understanding this, that the law is not laid down for the just but for the lawless and disobedient, for the ungodly and sinners, for the unholy and profane, for those who strike their fathers and mothers, for murderers, the sexually immoral, men who practice homosexuality, enslavers, liars, perjurers, and whatever else is contrary to sound doctrine. (1 Tim. 1:8–10; see also Matt. 19:8)

The Law, like a guardian or a tutor, was added because of Israel's transgression in order to protect them from the dangers and consequences of sin and unbelief until the Messiah comes. Now that the Messiah has come and made a new covenant, we (all followers of Yeshua) are no longer under the authority of the tutor.

The Law as Shadow

Another function of the Law as Scripture is to point to things pertaining to the Messiah and the new covenant. This truth is most clearly explained in the Epistle to the Hebrews.

> Now the point in what we are saying is this: we have such a high priest, one who is seated at the right hand of the throne of the Majesty in heaven, a minister in the holy places, in the true tent that the Lord set up, not man. For every high priest is appointed to offer gifts and sacrifices; thus it is necessary for this priest also to have something to offer. Now if he were on earth, he would not be a priest at all, since there are priests who offer gifts according to the law. They serve a copy and shadow of the heavenly things. For when Moses was about to erect the tent, he was instructed by God, saying, "See that you make everything according to the pattern that

was shown you on the mountain." (Heb. 8:1–5; see also Exod. 25:40)

How did the author of Hebrews come to this conclusion? By read-ing the Torah! On five occasions the Torah tells us the tabernacle is a copy (Exod. 25:9; 25:40; 26:30; 27:8; Num. 8:4). Though the Torah does not state explicitly that the earthly tabernacle is a copy of heav-enly realities, this truth is clearly implied both in the Torah and elsewhere in the Hebrew Scriptures. We are told, for instance, that when the tabernacle is completed, God's glory moves into the Holy of Holies (Exod. 40:34–38; see Lev. 1:1; 1 Kings 8:27). But this truth creates a bit of a theological dilemma since Deuteronomy 4:39 also teaches that the Lord God dwells not only on earth but also in heav-en above. Similarly, when God's glory fills the temple Solomon has built (1 Kings 8:11), the king offers a prayer beseeching God "to hear in heaven your dwelling place" (1 Kings 8:39; see vv. 32, 34, 36, 45, 49; 2 Chron. 6:27). So where does God actually dwell? In the tab-ernacle/temple? Yes! Solomon's prayer underscores the truth that God's true and lasting dwelling is not on earth since the tabernacle/temple can be destroyed. Therefore, the earthly tabernacle/temple must only be a replica, a copy, of the heavenly reality. Remarkably, Solomon even acknowledges that true forgiveness for sins takes place, not in the earthly sanctuary but in heaven (1 Kings 8:34, 36; 2 Chron. 6:27).

The Torah contains other clues suggesting that the tabernacle is only a copy of true realities. Earlier we discussed the parallels be-tween the garden of Eden and the tabernacle. For instance, the en-trance to the garden of Eden, like the tabernacle, is on the east, and is guarded by cherubim (Gen. 3:24; Exod. 26:1, 31), with one huge difference. The cherubim guarding the entrance to the tabernacle are copies; the cherubim guarding the garden are the real thing (see Ezek. 10:20).

Since the tabernacle is a copy of heavenly realities, it is divinely in-tended and properly understood as a witness to heavenly (messianic) realities. In fact, the author of Hebrews is quite clear on this point when he writes,

By this the Holy Spirit indicates that the way into the holy places is not yet opened as long as the first section is still standing (which is symbolic for the present age).[3] According to this arrangement, gifts and sacrifices are offered that cannot perfect the conscience of the worshiper, but deal only with food and drink and various washings, regulations for the body imposed until the time of reformation (Heb. 9:8–10).

Keeping the food laws of Leviticus 11 is an essential component of what people mean when they speak of "Torah observance" today. What people often fail to see, however, and what the writer of Hebrews so perceptively observes, is the connection between the food laws and the tabernacle. Leviticus 11 is part of a larger section in Leviticus (Lev. 11–15) called the Laws of Purity, all of which are tied to the purity of the tabernacle (Lev. 16). Beyond the fact that there is no longer a functioning tabernacle/temple, followers of Yeshua now are themselves the temple of the Holy Spirit (1 Cor. 3:16), the purity of which is no longer contingent upon following the Laws of Purity in Leviticus 11–15, but upon the final and perfect sacrifice of the Messiah Yeshua. Yeshua has fulfilled all the Laws of Purity for us, including the food laws! For this reason, both Paul and the writer of Hebrews are able to declare to Yeshua's followers, both Jewish and Gentile, that all foods are clean (Heb. 9:8–10; 13:9; 1 Tim. 4:1–5).

The continuous operation of the tabernacle with its sacrificial system, the Levitical priesthood, the ceremonial washings, etc. (i.e., the Sinai covenant), was specifically designed *not to last*. And as we meditate on the description of the tabernacle and its significance as found in Scripture for all believers today, its symbolism and built-in limitations are designed to point us to a better high priest, a better

---

3. The "present age" does not refer to the time of the writer of Hebrews since the author is writing about the tabernacle, not the temple. The "present age" refers to the age in which the tabernacle was in existence. See George H. Guthrie, *Hebrews,* NIV Application Commentary (Grand Rapids: Zondervan, 1998), 300.

sacrifice, and a better temple to which we now have direct access in Yeshua.

Elsewhere we also see that even the feasts are specifically designed with the Messiah in mind. "Therefore let no one pass judgment on you in questions of food and drink, or with regard to a festival or a new moon or a Sabbath. These are a shadow of the things to come, but the substance belongs to Christ" (Col. 2:16–17).

As followers of Yeshua, we want the Jewish people to see and to understand the substance of these shadows. And though we are no longer under the authority of the Sinai covenant and thus are no longer bound to keep the laws concerning the feasts,[4] we still seek to find ways to flesh out these fuller realities to the Jewish people. For those of us who are Jewish believers in Yeshua, particularly in Israel, the celebration of the feast days (Shabbat, Passover, Sukkot, etc.) affords us a great opportunity to show our people how the Law points to Yeshua.

Before we move on to our next point, let us address a matter about the Law that can easily be overlooked. The shadows in the Law continue to function as divine Scripture that not only points to the Messiah but also helps us to understand him. Without the Law, we would not understand the importance of sacrifices, the need for an intercessor or redeemer, the presentation of Yeshua as the Passover Lamb, and so on. Sadly, many followers of Yeshua feel they can throw the shadows aside now that the realities have come. This attitude often results in a failure to carefully study the Law as divinely inspired Scripture, written for the purpose of pointing to Yeshua. By neglecting the shadows, the realities are no longer properly understood, let alone appreciated. Let us not find ourselves as believers "who do not know Joseph" (Exod. 1:8), and consequently, "do not understand Yeshua"!

The Law as Theology

We have already looked at verses that clearly state that we are no longer under the Law, that is, under the old covenant. Again, Law here is

---

4. Leviticus 23 is filled with sacrificial prescriptions for the feast days. Even if we wanted to keep these laws, we could not since there is no longer a temple.

not to be confused with the Torah as a whole, as we have seen in our discussion of Galatians 3. But it is equally obvious that the whole of the Torah, including the Law, continues to function as Scripture for the writers of the New Testament. Peter, for example, encourages the believers to be holy since "he who called you is holy" (1 Peter 1:15). How does Peter know God is holy? Because this is what the Law teaches!

> As obedient children, do not be conformed to the passions of your former ignorance, but as he who called you is holy, you also be holy in all your conduct, since it is written, "You shall be holy, for I am holy." (1 Peter 1:14–16)

Here Peter makes his point by citing Leviticus 11:44: "For I am the LORD your God. Consecrate yourselves therefore, and be holy, for I am holy. You shall not defile yourselves with any swarming thing that crawls on the ground." The irony of the citation is obvious in the context of our discussion, since Peter is quoting the theological exhortation originally intended to motivate the people of Israel not to defile themselves with unclean food. The writer of Hebrews has made it quite clear that "food and drink and various washings, regulations for the body" were "imposed until the time of reformation" (Heb. 9:10). It is clear that Peter's point in the context is not to encourage his readers to follow the food laws but to "not be conformed to the passions of your former ignorance" (1 Peter 1:14).

So what are we to make of this? How can Peter derive unchanging theological truths from a passage whose laws, though still functioning as Scripture, are no longer binding upon his readers? The answer is straightforward: although Yeshua's non-Levitical priesthood requires a change in the Law (Heb. 7:12), the Law reflects the character of a God who never changes (Mal. 3:6). Though our expression of God's holiness may be different under the new covenant, God will always be holy (1 Peter 1:16; see Lev. 11:44–45). Likewise, just as it has been revealed in the Law, God will always be one (Mark 12:29; James 2:19; see also Deut. 6:4), and God will always be compassionate and merciful (Luke 6:36; James 5:11; see also Exod. 34:6, etc.).

Since God does not change and the Law is an expression of the character of God, the Law continues to function as theology—as the revelation of the person and character of God. We study and meditate on the Law in order to know more about the God who gave it, the God who ultimately gave his Son!

The Law as Love

When Yeshua is asked about the greatest commandment, he sums it all up in two:

> "Teacher, which is the great commandment in the Law?" And he said to him, "You shall love the Lord your God with all your heart and with all your soul and with all your mind. This is the great and first commandment. And a second is like it: You shall love your neighbor as yourself. On these two commandments depend all the Law and the Prophets." (Matt. 22:36–40)

The heart of all the commandments is love: loving God and loving others. Paul is clear on this point when he writes,

> Owe no one anything except to love each other, for the one who loves another has fulfilled the law. For the commandments, "You shall not commit adultery, You shall not murder, You shall not steal, You shall not covet," and any other commandment, are summed up in this word: "You shall love your neighbor as yourself." Love does no wrong to a neighbor; therefore love is the fulfilling of the law. (Rom. 13:8–10)

By meditating on the Law, we are reminded and challenged to live a life dedicated to loving God and loving others. By loving God and others, we fulfill the Law (see Matt. 5:17–48; James 2:10–12). This is not to say our love for God and people is expressed in the same ways it was under the old covenant. In some cases, our behavior as followers of Yeshua exceeds the written requirements of the Law (see, e.g., Matt. 5:27–28, 33–37). In other cases, our new covenant love is expressed in a manner that is contrary to the Law of Moses. When the writer of Hebrews tells his Jewish readers, regardless of their tribe, "to enter the holy places by the blood of Jesus, by the new and living way that he opened for us through the curtain, that is through his flesh" (Heb. 10:19–20), we are obviously encouraged to love God by approaching him in a manner that was strictly prohibited under the Law. When Paul encourages his Gentile (and Jewish) readers to celebrate the festival (Passover), "not with the old leaven, the leaven of malice and evil, but with the unleavened bread of sincerity and truth" (1 Cor. 5:8), he is clearly not concerned about the fact that the Law strictly forbids uncircumcised Gentiles from celebrating this festival (Exod. 12:48). Thus we see that loving God and people continues to be the heart of new covenant behavior, and that by loving we fulfill the Law. Yet we also see that our expression of love for God and people is not necessarily the same as it is under the Law.

The Law as Wisdom

As far as Paul is concerned, the Law (and the Torah as a whole) was written for us! On two occasions Paul quotes Deuteronomy 25:4, "You shall not muzzle an ox when it is treading out the grain," and applies it to the way we treat ministers of the new covenant (1 Cor. 9:9; 1 Tim. 5:18). In his words:

> Do I say these things on human authority? Does not the Law say the same? For it is written in the Law of Moses, "You shall not muzzle an ox when it treads out the grain." Is it for oxen that God is concerned? Does he not certainly speak for our sake? It was written for our sake, because the plowman should plow in hope and the thresher thresh in hope of sharing in the crop (1 Cor. 9:8–10).

The Law was not written for the sake of oxen, but for our sake! Similarly Paul writes in 1 Corinthians 10:9–11:

> We must not put Christ to the test, as some of them did and were destroyed by serpents, nor grumble, as some of

them did and were destroyed by the Destroyer. Now these things happened to them as an example, but they were written down for our instruction, on whom the end of the ages has come.

The tragic story of the fiery serpents was "written down for our instruction" (see also Eph. 6:1–3). Wait a minute! Earlier we saw that Paul regarded the Law as a tutor, set in place temporarily until the coming of Yeshua (Gal. 3:24). Elsewhere Paul states quite emphatically that we are no longer under the Law (Rom. 6:14; 7:1–4). So how can he say the laws were written for us if we are no longer under the Law? The answer to this question is found in Deuteronomy 4:5–6:

> See, I have taught you statutes and rules, as the LORD my God commanded me, that you should do them in the land that you are entering to take possession of it. Keep them and do them, for that will be your wisdom and your understanding in the sight of the peoples, who, when they hear all these statutes, will say, "Surely this great nation is a wise and understanding people."

The Law is an expression of God's great wisdom. In fact, the statutes and rules are identified as "your wisdom and your understanding." Paul's application of Deuteronomy 25:4 ("you shall not muzzle an ox") to the way we should treat ministers is a "wisdom application" based on *qal vahomer*.[5] If God commanded us to be kind and generous to animals who are producing physical food for us, how much kinder and more generous should we be to ministers who provide spiritual nourishment for us? Paul looks to the story of Israel's grumbling in the wilderness for wisdom in the present age. The Torah is clear that we should not grumble! When God tells the ancient Israelites to "make a parapet for your roof, that you may not bring the guilt of blood upon your house, if anyone should fall from

---

5. *Qal vahomer* is a rabbinic interpretive method that makes an argument from lesser to greater, such as in Matthew 6:30: "But if God so clothes the grass of the field, . . . will he not much more clothe you?"

it" (Deut. 22:8), we can draw forth principles for making our homes, offices, and so on safe for those who are in them. One obvious application of Deuteronomy 22:8 is the wisdom of "childproofing" our homes when we know there will be small children crawling around on the floors.[6] We meditate on the stories in the Torah as well as its laws to gain wisdom for living.

The Law as Prosecuting Attorney

In addition to the other purposes of the Law, we also see that the Law was divinely intended to testify against us.

> Moses commanded the Levites who carried the ark of the covenant of the LORD, "Take this Book of the Law and put it by the side of the ark of the covenant of the LORD your God, that it may be there for a witness against you." (Deut. 31:25–26)

The Law serves as a prosecuting attorney that testifies against us on a personal as well as on a national level.

> Now we know that whatever the law says it speaks to those who are under the law, so that every mouth may be stopped, and the whole world may be held accountable to God. For by works of the law no human being will be justified in his sight, since through the law comes knowledge of sin. (Rom. 3:19–20)

By meditating on the Law, we become aware of a problem that the Law itself was not ultimately designed to fix. By meditating on the Law, we become acutely aware of our need for lasting atonement, for the Messiah Yeshua.

---

6. This is precisely how it seems most "Law" was given in the ancient Near East (as, e.g., Hammurabi). It was not given as civil law per se, but rather, as the set of rulings of a wise king. These rulings were copied over and over again as guidelines for wise rulings. Hence their application became practical for subsequent generations. Thus sometimes when the New Testament writer quotes the Old Testament, he does not change the meaning as it might appear but is perhaps quoting it to draw attention to the principle behind it.

But now the righteousness of God has been manifested apart from the law, although the Law and the Prophets bear witness to it—the righteousness of God through faith in Jesus Christ for all who believe. For there is no distinction: for all have sinned and fall short of the glory of God, and are justified by his grace as a gift, through the redemption that is in Christ Jesus, whom God put forward as a propitiation by his blood, to be received by faith. This was to show God's righteousness, because in his divine forbearance he had passed over former sins. It was to show his righteousness at the present time, so that he might be just and the justifier of the one who has faith in Jesus. (Rom. 3:21–26)

A controversial and oft-misunderstood passage of Scripture bears examining here as an illustration of how the apostle Paul views his relationship to the Law. In Acts 21:20–26, Paul goes to the temple to purify himself and four men and to make an offering, according to the Law of Moses. Some suggest that Paul's animal sacrifice is proof that he was under the Law. However, context is everything. It should be noted that ceremonial "purification" did not necessarily involve atonement for personal sin. Women had to be "purified" following the birth of a child (Lev. 12:2; Luke 2:22), even though the act of bearing a child is not sinful. Paul's act of "purification," therefore, need not suggest that he was seeking personal forgiveness by means of an animal sacrifice.

What then is going on in these verses? Here was the problem: a report had been circulated widely that Paul went about constantly teaching that Jews, especially those who lived in Gentile lands, should "forsake" (*apostasia*, cf. apostatize) Moses, meaning the Law. Paul is being accused of heresy. How can the believers in Jerusalem demonstrate to an extremely religious population that Paul is in fact an obedient Israelite, without entering into endless explanations, arguments, and a possible uproar? They find the answer in the Nazarite vow. No law will be violated if Paul joins in this dedication service, for the temple and the authorized priesthood are both present. Indeed, much will be gained from a silent public display of obedience. So Paul, as a gesture of goodwill, agrees to their plan and rededicates himself to God along with the others. The apostle Paul joins in a dedication service to dispel doubts and rumors for the same reason he has Timothy circumcised: "because of the Jews who were in those places" (Acts 16:3). As Paul himself says: "To the Jews I became as a Jew, in order to win Jews. To those under the law I became as one under the law (though not being myself under the law) that I might win those under the law" (1 Cor. 9:20).

Paul goes beyond stating he is not under the Law by arguing that his former life under the Law was radically changed when he met Yeshua. He writes:

> If anyone else thinks he has reason for confidence in the flesh, I have more: circumcised on the eighth day, of the people of Israel, of the tribe of Benjamin, a Hebrew of Hebrews; as to the law, a Pharisee; as to zeal, a persecutor of the church; as to righteousness under the law, blameless. But whatever gain I had, I counted as loss for the sake of Christ. Indeed, I count everything as loss because of the surpassing worth of knowing Christ Jesus my Lord. For his sake I have suffered the loss of all things and count them as rubbish, in order that I may gain Christ and be found in him, not having a righteousness of my own that comes from the law, but that which comes through faith in Christ, the righteousness from God that depends on faith—that I may know him and the power of his resurrection. (Phil. 3:4–10)

We realize the Law is good and holy and beautiful. The Law, as part of the Torah story as a whole, continues to function as inspired Scripture that teaches, informs, and instructs (2 Tim. 3:16–17). We are aware that there are probably more answers to the question why the Law? But these few should suffice to show that just because we claim that Yeshua (rather than the Law) is the goal of the Torah, we are not throwing the Law out the window as passé and useless. We are rather putting it in the place God always intended for it to be from the beginning: as a tutor, as a shadow, as theology, as love, as wisdom, and as a testimony against us that all have fallen short of the glory of God and need to look elsewhere for the solution to our inability to keep the Law.

CHAPTER 10

God's Compromised Ideals

Dr. Laura Schlessinger is an observant Orthodox Jew and a US radio personality who gives Torah-based advice to people who call in to her radio show. The following response is an open letter to Laura Schlesinger—saturated with sarcasm—that went viral on the Internet.

> Dear Dr. Laura:
>
> Thank you for doing so much to educate people regarding God's Law. I have learned a great deal from your show, and try to share that knowledge with as many people as I can. When someone tries to defend the homosexual lifestyle, for example, I simply remind them that Leviticus 18:22 clearly states it to be an abomination. . . End of debate.
>
> I do need some advice from you, however, regarding some other elements of God's Laws and how to follow them.
>
> 1. Leviticus 25:44 states that I may possess slaves, both male and female, provided they are purchased from neighboring nations. A friend of mine claims that this applies to Mexicans, but not Canadians. Can you clarify? Why can't I own Canadians?
>
> 2. I would like to sell my daughter into slavery, as sanctioned in Exodus 21:7. In this day and age, what do you think would be a fair price for her?
>
> 3. I know that I am allowed no contact with a woman while she is in her period of menstrual uncleanliness—Leviticus 15:

19–24. The problem is how do I tell? I have tried asking, but most women take offense.

4. When I burn a bull on the altar as a sacrifice, I know it creates a pleasing odor for the Lord— Leviticus 1:9. The problem is, my neighbors. They claim the odor is not pleasing to them. Should I smite them?

5. I have a neighbor who insists on working on the Sabbath. Exodus 35:2 clearly states he should be put to death. Am I morally obligated to kill him myself, or should I ask the police to do it?

6. A friend of mine feels that even though eating shellfish is an abomination— Leviticus 11:10, it is a lesser abomination than homosexuality. I don't agree. Can you settle this? Are there "degrees" of abomination?

7. Leviticus 21:20 states that I may not approach the altar of God if I have a defect in my sight. I have to admit that I wear reading glasses. Does my vision have to be 20/20, or is there some wiggle-room here?

8. Most of my male friends get their hair trimmed, including the hair around their temples, even though this is expressly forbidden by Leviticus 19:27. How should they die?

9. I know from Leviticus 11:6–8 that touching the skin of a dead pig makes me unclean, but may I still play football if I wear gloves?

10. My uncle has a farm. He violates Leviticus 19:19 by planting two different crops in the same field, as does his wife by wearing garments made of two different kinds of thread (cotton/polyester blend). He also tends to curse and blaspheme a lot. Is it really necessary that we go to all the trouble of getting the whole town together to stone them? (Lev. 24:10–16). Couldn't we just burn them to death at a private family affair, like we do with people who sleep with their in-laws? (Lev. 20:14)

I know you have studied these things extensively and thus enjoy considerable expertise in such matters, so I am confident you can help. Thank you again for reminding us that God's word is eternal and unchanging.

Your devoted disciple and adoring fan.

This letter raises the question: though we know that the Law is spiritual (Rom. 7:14), aren't the laws in the Torah primitive? Well, in a sense, yes!

Let's jump a few thousand years back to the time of the ancient Near East, a culture and mindset completely foreign to ours today whose social structures are badly damaged by the Fall. Within this context, God raises up a new nation with new laws to live by, in order to create a new culture for them. In doing so, he adapts his expectations to a people whose attitudes and actions are subject to influence by the pagan nations around them. These laws aren't the permanent, divine ideal for all peoples everywhere at all times. They are specific to that people with their specific needs in that ancient era. As we saw earlier, the Hebrew Bible considers the Mosaic Law to be inferior, looking toward a future and better covenant (Jer. 31; Ezek. 36). It's not that the Mosaic Law is bad and therefore needs to be replaced. The Law is good (Rom. 7:12), but it is only a less-than-ideal temporary measure. It is in fact a compromise on God's part.

Take for example God's ideal for marriage—a monogamous union joining husband and wife as one flesh (Gen. 2:24). When God is dealing with Israel, a nation of fallen humans affected by their surroundings in the ancient Near East, God's ideals are distorted and forgotten. Therefore, God is on the move to restore his ideals through this small new nation. The laws of Moses are a first step in that process.

Baby Steps

Let's take a look at where God chooses to show up. He chooses a fallen culture of patriarchal structures, primogeniture, polygamy, warfare, slavery, and other fallen human and social behaviors, which God allows temporarily to exist because of the hardness of the human heart. As Jesus states in Matthew 19:8, "Because of your hardness of heart Moses allowed you to divorce your wives, but from the beginning it was not so." We could apply this passage to all the "weird laws" in the Torah, such as those brought up by Dr. Laura's sardonic letter-writer. The bottom line is, God meets Israel where they live. "Because of your hardness of heart," God through Moses permits slavery, patriarchy, warfare, and on and on. "But from the beginning it was not so."

The laws of Moses are not ideal nor universal. The New Testament acknowledges that God put up with inferior social and human behavior, that "in his divine forbearance he had passed over former sins" (Rom. 3:25). Previously, "the times of ignorance God overlooked, but now he commands all people everywhere to repent" (Acts 17:30).

God works with Israel's human fallenness, while taking them with baby steps toward his holy ideal. Therefore, the Sinai legislation makes moral improvements without completely overriding the social structures of their ancient Near Eastern cultural context. At the same time God seeks to show them a higher ideal. As one professor of biblical studies puts it, "If human beings are to be treated as real human beings who possess the power of choice, then the 'better way' must come gradually. Otherwise, they will exercise their freedom of choice and turn away from what they do not understand."[1] Hebrews 7:18 states, "A former commandment is set aside because of its weakness and uselessness (for the law made nothing perfect)."

God, loving and gracious as he is, brings about moral improvement and a movement toward restoring the pre-Fall ideals. In fact, comparing Moses' laws with those of Israel's ancient neighbors, we see dramatic moral improvements over the barbarian practices of the other surrounding Near Eastern nations and cultures.

So when we come across stories such as Joshua 10:22–27, where Joshua hangs the corpses of five Canaanite kings on trees all day, we don't have to explain them away or justify them. Joshua's actions remind us of the moral condition of the culture of his time. They also remind us that God can use heroes such as Joshua within their context and work out his redemptive purposes despite their shortcomings.

An Example of Progress: Slavery

Taking a "bird's eye view" of humanity's progress across the timeline of the Scriptures, we can see how the status of slaves, for example, gradually changes from degradation to a restoration of human dignity.

---

1. Alden Thompson, *Who's Afraid of the Old Testament God?* (Grand Rapids: Zondervan, 1988), 33.

In ancient Near Eastern culture, treatment of slaves is brutal and demeaning. Slaves do not have the value of other human beings. They have no rights and are subject to corporal punishment and are even put to death without regard for their humanity.

Moses' laws regarding slaves, while far from ideal, bring a big improvement over the ancient Near Eastern culture: punishments are limited. There is a more humanized attitude toward slaves. Runaway foreign slaves are given refuge in Israel (Deut. 23:15–16), versus being put to death as they would be in the surrounding cultures.[2] We should also point out that slavery in the Bible never approximated American slavery, with its denial of full personhood.

The New Testament provides further improvement over Moses' laws: Christian slaves in the Roman Empire are considered equal to their masters in the body of Christ (Gal. 3:28). Masters are to take care of their slaves, and slaves are encouraged to seek freedom (1 Cor. 7:20–22).

God's ideals are already in place at creation, but God accommodates himself to human hard-heartedness and the social structures of a fallen world. The ancient Near East displays a deviation from these ideals. Incremental "baby steps" are given to Old Testament Israel that tolerate certain moral deficiencies, while encouraging Israel to strive toward a new and better ideal.

---

2. Paul Copan, *Is God a Moral Monster? Making Sense of the Old Testament God* (Grand Rapids: Baker, 2011), 63.

CHAPTER 11

Moses' Law Today?

Keeping the Law Is Impossible

What if Israel really wanted to continue observing the Law? Well, it is simply impossible. There is no longer a priesthood, no temple, and no sacrificial system—all of which comprise the heart and essence of the Law. We cannot separate the Sinai covenant from the Law. The laws are merely an outgrowth of the covenant; they cannot stand on their own, just as eating mayonnaise and mustard is pointless without the rest of the sandwich. The Sinai covenant was ratified by the shedding of blood (Exod. 24:8) and was maintained by the blood of the sacrifices upon the altar (Exod. 30:10). Without the sacrificial system we are unable to keep the Sinai covenant. Those who want to can only pick out a few laws to keep that are not related to the temple, the priesthood, or the sacrificial system. Moreover, while these laws continue to speak to us as inspired Scripture, as we saw previously, many of them were given to Israel 3,500 years ago in order to establish a nation in the context of the ancient Near Eastern world. If we were to establish a new nation today, we would give its people laws and rules (regarding traffic, family, taxes, torts, rights, labor, etc.) according to their situation, lifestyle, era, and location. However, many of Moses' laws are practically impossible to keep in our day and age, due to the current reality in which we live—for example, issues concerning slavery or purification rituals are no longer relevant.

In modern terms, suggesting that Israel (or anyone for that matter) can be justified and saved by keeping the Law is like giving someone an old laptop without its motherboard or processor. Even though the laptop might be able to perform a few functions such as typing on the keyboard, there is no point without the key components of motherboard and processor. The key component of the Sinai covenant is the blood of the covenant. Indeed, God has a new, upgraded laptop to give us as a free gift, sufficient for all our needs!

Have you ever asked yourself, "What if there were a temple today? Would Israel be able to keep the Sinai covenant and be saved by the Law?" The answer is still no. First, the temple records, which included the priestly genealogies, were all destroyed with the destruction of the Second Temple. Therefore, even if there were a temple today, there is no way for us to be certain of who should serve as priest. Second, we now have a new covenant: those who are in Yeshua are a new creation. God's new and more complete revelation allows the old to pass away. In the new covenant, *we* are now the temple: "Do you not know that you are God's temple and that God's Spirit dwells in you?" (1 Cor. 3:16).

Confirmation in the Talmud

The Talmud is a collection of ancient traditional, non-biblical Jewish writings comprised of rabbinic commentary on the Law of Moses. Although we do not accept the authority of the Talmud as a document inspired by God, not only is it possible to learn a lot about the Second Temple period from it but we also can see that, perhaps without intending to, the sages of the Talmud (ancient rabbis) corroborate the New Testament's declaration that the old covenant is no longer functioning. According to the Talmud, when the Second Temple was still standing, the high priest would set himself apart for a week prior to Yom Kippur (the Day of Atonement) to prepare himself spiritually. During the Day of Atonement he would not sleep, but would make sacrifices—for himself first, and then for the nation of Israel. Simultaneously, the people of Israel would fast, pray, and repent of the national sins before God. It was the blood on the altar that temporarily covered the national sins for another year (Lev. 17:11).

Now we get to the interesting part. The Talmud says that at the end of that day the high priest would wait for God's "miraculous stamp of approval," indicating the acceptance of Israel's atonement. How would God show his approval? According to the Talmud, inside the temple there was a red fabric (*lashon shel ze'hurit*). This piece of fabric would miraculously turn from red to white as a sign to the nation that God had indeed accepted their sacrifice and that their sins would be covered for one more year. The sages write (see Tractate *Yoma* 39b) that forty years prior to the destruction of the temple in Jerusalem (around AD 30, since the temple was destroyed in AD 70), the red fabric stopped turning white on the Day of Atonement.[1] The Talmud explains that this caused much panic and distress among the priests.

From around the year AD 30, according to the Talmud, God no longer honored the Sinai covenant as the way to cover Israel's sins. What happened to the Sinai covenant? The answer is that the Law is now fulfilled in a new way—not by something that will temporarily cover our sins for a year, but by Someone who atones for our sins once and for all:

> For it is impossible for the blood of bulls and goats to take away sins. Consequently, when Christ came into the world, he said, "Sacrifices and offerings you have not desired, but a body have you prepared for me." . . . And by that will we have been sanctified through the offering of the body of Jesus Christ once for all. (Heb. 10:4–5, 10)

Jewish Identity Crisis

In the period following the destruction of the temple in AD 70, the Jewish religious leadership faced a serious problem. Unlike the first Diaspora that would last for seventy years according to God's revelation through Jeremiah, there was now no prophecy with a specific time limit that they could perceive. How could the Jewish nation continue to exist without a temple, with God's rejection of their sacrificial system, and without the Messiah? The gravity of the Jewish identity crisis of this moment in history cannot be overstated. Yet,

---

1. See also *Rosh HaShanah* 31b and 32a. There are also similar references in the Mishna and in the Yerushalmi.

the words of the prophet Jeremiah should have alleviated their panic and distress:

> Behold, the days are coming, declares the LORD, when I will make a new covenant with the house of Israel and the house of Judah, not like the covenant that I made with their fathers on the day when I took them by the hand to bring them out of the land of Egypt, my covenant that they broke, though I was their husband, declares the LORD. For this is the covenant that I will make with the house of Israel after those days, declares the LORD: I will put my law within them, and I will write it on their hearts. (Jer. 31:31–33)

What started as a spiritual revival around the word of God in the days of Ezra and Nehemiah grew to be a movement idealizing applicational traditions: Pharisaic tradition was evolving into rabbinic Judaism. Declaring man-made traditions to be the way, the truth, and the life was not a new idea, as we read in Isaiah 29:13: "This people draw near with their mouth and honor me with their lips, while their hearts are far from me, and their fear of me is a commandment taught by men." Justification for giving such authority to these human traditions was made by claiming they had actually been given to Moses at Mount Sinai as the Oral Law. In the sixty-five-year formative period between that critical year AD 70 and AD 135, Judaism became a religion whose authority was invested in the rabbis, rather than in the divine revelation of the ancient Hebrew Scriptures. The leaders of the Jewish world in that formative period intentionally disconnected from the Bible. This might sound harsh, but it is actually what the Talmud itself teaches. There is a famous and foundational story in the Talmud, demonstrating the new authority claimed by the Pharisaic leadership that took over the Jewish world. This story concerns an argument between the famous rabbis Eliezer ben Hyrkanus and Joshua ben Hananiah about "Akhnai's Oven" (*Baba Metzia* 59b).

The argument has to do with a question raised by a man named Akhnai, a baker who had an oven made of clay. His baking business was expanding, and he enlarged the oven by cutting it to pieces and then joining the pieces with sand to create a larger oven. The question he brought before the Sanhedrin was whether the new oven is clean (kosher) or unclean (a key question for Akhnai in terms of his business). The Talmud details that Rabbi Eliezer brought "all the answers in the world" to prove the oven is indeed clean, but the majority of rabbis, from another school of thought, do not accept his answers and claim it is not clean. Rabbi Eliezer began trying to prove with supernatural signs that he was right—a fig tree was miraculously plucked up by its roots and replanted on the other side of the yard, the water in an aqueduct runs uphill, and so on. To all these, the majority of rabbis refused to pay attention and kept to the opposing position. Finally, Rabbi Eliezer called out, "If I am right, the heavens will prove it!" Then God spoke audibly from heaven (*bat-kol*), and said, "My son Eliezer is correct"! Immediately, Rabbi Joshua, the leader opposing Rabbi Eliezer, made one of the most significant declarations in the Talmud: *"It is not in Heaven!"* (a phrase taken out of context from Deut. 30:12). By this Rabbi Joshua was saying that God no longer makes decisions in heaven; rather, the rabbis make them on earth. Rabbi Joshua pronounced that God gave us (i.e., the rabbis representing Israel) his word, and therefore now it is ours to interpret as we please.[2]

The Talmud goes on to say that following all these happenings, Elijah the prophet and Moses asked the Holy One, blessed be His name, "What just happened?" God smiled and responded, "My sons have been victorious over me," meaning that God accepts the rabbis' authority to be greater than that of the Scriptures and greater even than himself. Or, in Rabbi Joshua's own words at the end of this Talmudic passage, "The Torah itself is to be uncovered not by prophets, nor even by God's miracles or audible voice, but by man's interpretation and decision making."

---

2. We see a good example of interpreting "as we please" with another of Rabbi Joshua's famous sayings: "Turn aside after a multitude," by which he means that the majority rules. He is quoting Exodus 23:2 in the exact opposite sense of what that verse actually means, as can clearly be seen by reading the whole verse: "You shall not fall in with the many (or turn aside after a multitude) to do evil, . . . so as to pervert justice."

This Talmudic story sharply demonstrates the dramatic change that began to take place in the Jewish world from that period, even until now Jews are no longer under the authority of God's word, but rather under independent, creative, and man-made interpretation and application. From that point on, rabbinical tradition has been called the Oral Law, and is "canonized" in the Talmud, which is comprised of the Mishna and Gemara. It is imperative to understand the magnitude and breadth of the change that the Jewish world underwent, when we come to talk about keeping or adhering to Jewish tradition, which is sometimes erroneously referred to as Torah. Paul, in fact, speaks of Israel's zeal to establish a righteousness through man-made rules:

> Brothers, my heart's desire and prayer to God for them is that they may be saved. For I bear them witness that they have a zeal for God, but not according to knowledge. For, being ignorant of the righteousness of God, and seeking to establish their own, they did not submit to God's righteousness. For Christ is the end of the law for righteousness to everyone who believes." (Rom. 10:1–4)

What Is Moses' Seat?

Some of you might be wondering: Are you sure we should not follow the Oral Law? After all, didn't Yeshua himself tell us to listen to the rabbis and follow their laws in Matthew 23:2–3, which says, "The scribes and the Pharisees sit on Moses' seat, so do and observe whatever they tell you"?

It is not wise to build a comprehensive and wide-reaching theology upon a single verse, especially one taken out of context. At this point in Matthew's Gospel, Yeshua is speaking *before* the new covenant has been established. After all, if Yeshua wanted us to follow the rabbis (Pharisees and scribes), he would mention it somewhere else in the Gospels. Neither do the apostles teach us to follow the rabbis. Yeshua demonstrates in his own life the exact opposite of this. He does not wash his hands according to the tradition of the Second Temple period (Matt. 15:1–9). Elsewhere he clearly states: "You have a fine way of rejecting the commandment of God in order to establish your tradition!" (Mark 7:9). The idea that God despises man-made religious traditions as a means to gain his favor is not new. We see it throughout the Bible (Isa. 29:13).

Therefore, if Yeshua is suggesting in a single verse that we must obey the rabbis, he forgot to inform us which rabbinical sect to follow (e.g., the house of Shammai or the house of Hillel), for they represented opposing interpretations of the Law in Yeshua's day. Furthermore, Yeshua would be in direct contradiction with the prophets and even with his own teaching in the same chapter, as we will see!

So what is Yeshua talking about in this verse? Does "Moses' seat" refer to rabbinic authority as some have argued? No! Rather, "Moses' seat" refers to the physical place in the synagogue where the Scriptures are read.

If we were living in the Second Temple period in Israel, we would not have our own copy of the Hebrew Scriptures, nor would there be any bookstores or Internet. How would we, as Second Temple period Jews, become exposed to the Hebrew Scriptures? There is only one way: we would have to go to a synagogue. It is at the synagogue— from "Moses' seat"—that the Hebrew Scriptures are read. Support for this interpretation can be found in a village north of the Sea of Galilee called Chorazin (just ninety minutes from our Bible College). In an ancient synagogue dating from the fourth century, archaeologists have discovered something called "Moses' seat," a seat in the synagogue where the Hebrew Scriptures were read aloud. Though the inscriptions at this site are from a later period, it is safe to assume this custom did not suddenly appear out of the blue in the fourth century. This is also affirmed by the Talmud Department of Bar-Ilan University.[3]

When Yeshua tells the people of Israel to listen to the scribes and Pharisees when they read from Moses' seat, he means it in a literal way. And why is it so important to Yeshua that the people of Israel listen to the Scriptures being read? Yeshua knows that the Scriptures

---

3. Prof. Hananel Mack of Bar-Ilan University's Talmudic Department, in his paper, "The Seat of Moses," affirms that the New Testament's "Seat of Moses" is referring to the physical seat from which Scriptures were read inside the synagogue. He bases this both on modern archaeological findings and on the ancient rabbinic commentary *Pesikta de-Rab Kahana* 7b.

all point to him: "For if you believed Moses, you would believe me; for he wrote of me" (John 5:46). Moses' seat in the synagogue was the only place from which a Jewish person in the Second Temple period could hear Moses and the Prophets bear testimony concerning the Messiah: "The LORD your God will raise up for you a prophet like me from among you, from your brothers—it is to him you shall listen" (Deut. 18:15). *Yeshua wants the people of Israel to listen to Moses, because Moses points to him.*

Earlier we claimed that Yeshua would have been contradicting himself if he were in fact requiring us to obey the rabbis (Pharisees and scribes). In exactly the same chapter (Matt. 23), he accuses the Pharisees and scribes of being "hypocrites" (v. 13), "child[ren] of hell" (v. 15), "blind guides" (v. 16), "blind fools" (v. 17), "full of hypocrisy and lawlessness" (v. 28), "serpents" and "a brood of vipers" (v. 33), and murderers (v. 35). Do we seriously think Yeshua commands us to follow them? Yeshua clearly states that they are respecting man-made traditions over God's word! (Matt. 15:9, quoting Isa. 29:13). When Yeshua says, "The scribes and the Pharisees sit on Moses' seat, so do and observe whatever they tell you, *but not the works they do*" (Matt. 23:2–3, emphasis added), he is referring to those man-made traditions they promote in the name of God (later called the Oral Law). Matthew 23 in its entirety shows us that Yeshua opposes man-made religion and traditions as a way to reach God.

Additionally, if Yeshua were telling us to obey the scribes and Pharisees we would have an even bigger dilemma. For the Oral Law directly contradicts the teachings of Yeshua. The Talmud teaches not only that Yeshua is a false prophet but also that when supposedly contacted through sorcery after his death, Yeshua is asked about his fate. Yeshua allegedly replies that he is suffering in hell, "in boiling excrement" (*Gittin* 57). It simply makes no sense that Yeshua would ask us to give any credence to such teachings!

Flesh Versus Spirit

There is a further conceptual problem in the claim that Yeshua commands us to obey the traditions of men as a way of life. Yeshua speaks with razor-sharp precision: "That which is born of the flesh is flesh, and that which is born of the Spirit is spirit. . . . It is the

Spirit who gives life; the flesh [human acts or traditions] is no help at all" (John 3:6; 6:63). If we are going to worship and serve God in Spirit, we cannot be reconciled to God or please him through man-made traditions. For "God is Spirit, and those who worship him must worship in spirit and truth" (John 4:24). While there is nothing wrong in wearing a kippa (yarmulke), or laying tefillin, or separating meat from milk (rabbinic kosher), this cannot change our hearts, earn points with God, or help us to better love other people. Modern Judaism looks to the rabbinic traditions as the way to please God and be considered righteous before him. In this sense, we can see how these traditions remove Yeshua from his God-ordained place: the One who makes us righteous before God. Therefore, for all believers, Jew and Gentile, mandatory obedience to the rabbinic traditions does not represent the faith of our fathers, but a rejection of Yeshua our Messiah.

Following man-made laws or rabbinic traditions as believers not only misses the point of the Torah, but also confuses both believers and non-believers. We cannot become "more Jewish" or draw nearer to God by following human traditions. If we think we can, then we are seeing the purpose of the Torah through rabbinic Judaism's eyes and not through Yeshua's eyes. This is exactly why Paul questions the Jews and Gentiles of Galatia: "Are you so foolish? Having begun by the Spirit, are you now being perfected by the flesh?" (Gal. 3:3). [4] The Galatians, just like the sages of rabbinic Judaism, do not understand the purpose of the Law.

Where Does the Oral Law Come From?

The concept of a God-given Oral Law is a myth. An Oral Law was never given to Moses at Mount Sinai; it is 100 percent man-made, and

---

4. Some suggest Paul's letter to the Galatians is directed only to a Gentile audience, in that the Galatian churches were comprised of Gentiles alone. However, we believe this not to be the case for three reasons: (1) According to 1 Peter 1:1 there were clearly Jews in the Galatian church. (2) According to Josephus (Joseph ben Mattityahu AD 37–100) there were Jews in the city of Galatia. (3) Paul and Barnabas preached "to the Jew first and also to the Greek" (Rom. 1:16). Acts does not record a single incident of Paul's preaching to the Jewish people when at least some did not respond positively. The same pattern continues in the cities of Iconium, Lystra, and Derbe as well.

one can even claim that it a significant part of Israel's blindness and hardness of heart toward Yeshua to this day (Rom. 11:25). As long as people try to work out their own salvation by keeping man-made traditions, they fail to understand their need for the Savior. The Oral Law has been the main reason Yeshua is a prohibited, unknown person to Israel to this very day. But God can always be counted on to turn bitter into sweet! Though the Oral Law persisted during the last two thousand years as an apologetic against faith in Yeshua, this same Oral Law also served as an instrument in preserving Israel as a distinct nation. This is analogous to Israel's sojourn in Egypt, whereby God used Egypt's loathing of the Hebrews as a protective incubator to multiply the nation and to keep it from assimilating with the Egyptians.[5]

Let us delve deeper. As mentioned earlier, after the destruction of the Second Temple, without a functioning priesthood, altar, or sacrifices, the sages were desperate to find a way through which they could retain authority and thus hold the Jewish world together, but without Yeshua. They needed a Judaism that could continue to function without the temple and without the Messiah they had rejected. In other words, they had to establish their authority over the Jewish people, and the way to do it was to establish rabbinic traditions as the new law. This law gave the learned rabbis the authority and control over all religious and social aspects of the people of Israel, while annihilating any other Jewish tradition of the day (Sadducees, messianic, etc.). In order to convince the people of Israel of the authenticity of this *modus operandi*, the rabbis claimed that the Oral Law was actually given to Moses on Mount Sinai. For example, the Jewish philosopher Maimonides claims at the beginning of his introduction to the Mishnah (Tractate *Avot* 1:1) that Moses knows the entire Oral Law by heart, and that he imparts it to the wise men and to all the people. This sounds nice, but the truth is, as recorded four times in the Torah (Lev. 24:12; Num. 9:8; 15:34; 27:5), Moses himself does not know how to give an answer with regard to the commandments. In

---

5. Though God turns the bitter into sweet, we should not use this as an excuse to ignore our mandate to proclaim the gospel to the Jew first.

each of these instances, Moses refers the question to God and waits for his answer.

This indicates, despite Maimonides' claim, that Moses does not receive an Oral Law with a complete and detailed explanation on how to implement all the written laws in the Torah. The Scriptures clearly show that God's covenant with the people of Israel at Sinai is based only upon the written Law, which he commands Moses to write. In Exodus 34:27, God commands Moses: "Write these words, for in accordance with these words I have made a covenant with you and with Israel." No other law is mentioned, neither any Oral Law of unwritten tradition that was supposedly transmitted by word of mouth.

Yet the sages make the claim that the Oral Law was indeed part of God's impartation at Sinai. They come up with a new *drash* (a commentary or interpretation) on Exodus 34:27. The rabbis claim that when God says "in accordance with these words" (*al-pi*), it actually means "on the lips" (*l^{e}fi*), that is, the Oral Law. However, this theory of an Oral Law comes from a twisted interpretation of a Hebrew phrase, as we have seen previously in the discussion about Akhnai's oven. The most natural translation of this phrase in its context is "in accordance with," a translation that is supported by all other similar occurrences in the Torah (Gen. 43:7; Lev. 27:18; Num. 26:56; Deut. 17:10–11). This interpretation is also supported by all modern English translations of this passage, whether Christian or Jewish: "And the Lord said to Moses: write down these commandments, for in accordance with these commandments I make a covenant with you and with Israel."[6]

The Authority of the Book

No doubt, the Talmud is an impressive compilation of human knowledge and wisdom, but there is no historical or biblical basis whatsoever for the idea that the Oral Law was given to Moses on Mount Sinai. The contrary is true. If an Oral Law was given to Moses by God, you would expect to read about it throughout the Hebrew Bible. But neither God nor Moses ever mentions the term Oral Law,

---

6. *The New JPS Translation According to the Traditional Hebrew Text*, 1985.

nor do we see evidence of it in Scripture. Not even Joshua ben Nun, whom God appoints as Moses' successor, gives us any indication of an unwritten law. God says to Joshua,

> This Book of the Law shall not depart from your mouth, but you shall meditate on it day and night, so that you may be careful to do according to all that is written in it. For then you will make your way prosperous, and then you will have good success. (Josh. 1:8)

God tells Joshua he should do everything *written* in the Book of the Law. God gives no indication of an Oral Law passed on to Joshua from Moses. The case is the same with Ezra the scribe, and any prophet or king in the Hebrew Scriptures: no one ever mentions that term or implies the existence of such a God-given Oral Law. If an Oral Law did exist, it was not a part of God's covenant with Israel. None of the biblical writers expressed any interest in or desire to know or to obey any sort of Oral Law. In other words, based on what is actually written in the Hebrew Scriptures, an Oral Law that was given to Moses by God on Mount Sinai never existed. The term Oral Law actually appears for the very first time approximately 1,500 years after the time of Moses!

Interestingly, the Qumran (Dead Sea) scrolls and the Jewish Apocrypha (200–100 BC) never mention or even imply the existence of a God-given Oral Law. The Cyrus Cylinder (sixth century BC) that describes the Jews of Babylon and their lifestyle not only fails to mention any existence of a God-given Oral Law, but actually sheds light in the other direction. According to Irving Finkel, a prominent authority on the Cyrus Cylinder, Jewish identity was internal only, without any external religious markers. Another convincing proof comes from Ethiopia. According to their own traditions, the Jews of Ethiopia returned to Israel after thousands of years in exile and from relative isolation. These Ethiopian Jews did not recognize the authority of the rabbis. They did not recognize the rabbinic traditions, and they had never heard of the rabbis' invention of the Oral Law. *The Oral Law was never given to Moses on Mount Sinai. It was invented by the sages in order for Judaism to continue to exist under their exclusive authority, without the temple and without the Messiah whom they had rejected.*

This same agenda affects any believers who try to root their identity in man-made traditions. Identity should not be based in deeds or traditions. Our identity as believers, whether Jew or Gentile, must be rooted in Yeshua himself (Phil. 3:20). Tradition is not the problem in and of itself, but it should never dominate our walk with the Lord (see Phil. 3:4–8).

By now you have probably realized that there is no such thing as "Torah observant," since most of the commandments are impossible to keep even if we wanted to try. The commandments chosen to be observed are cherry picked, with most being ignored and only a few followed. If somebody tells you they are Torah observant, try randomly picking a few commandments to see if they truly observe them or not. For example, like Dr. Laura's correspondent, you might ask:

- Do you keep your diet 100 percent animal-fat free, in accordance with Leviticus 3:17?
- Do you stone your children if they curse you, in accordance with Leviticus 20:9?
- Do you refrain from shaving your facial hair, in accordance with Leviticus 19:27?
- Do you support the killing of gays and lesbians, in accordance with Leviticus 20:13?
- During Shabbat, do you refrain from driving, barbecuing, turning on your lights, or using heating during the winter, in accordance with Exodus 35:3?
- Do you only wear only one kind of fabric at a time, in accordance with Deuteronomy 22:11?
- Do you refrain from purchasing fruit in the supermarket, as their suppliers do not wait until the fifth year of production to begin selling in accordance with Leviticus 19:23–25?

These are only seven examples out of hundreds of Sinai commandments. And remember, if we are still under the authority of the Sinai covenant as followers of Yeshua, we cannot just keep some commandments, we must keep them all: "For whoever keeps the whole law but fails in one point has become guilty of all of it" (James 2:10).

Some in the Hebrew roots movement appeal to John 14:15 to support their position that Yeshua's followers are obligated to keep the Law: "If you love me, you will keep my commandments" (John 14:15; see 14:21, 23–24). There is absolutely nothing in the immediate context, however, which would lead one to conclude that "my commandments" refers to the Law. Biblical interpretation relies heavily on context, and the immediate context here clarifies the specific commandments to which Yeshua refers: "This is my commandment, that you love one another as I have loved you. . . . These things I command you, so that you will love one another" (John 15:12, 17). [7]

---

7. Other commandments given by Yeshua in the immediate context include John 14:1, 11, 27; 15:4, 7, 9; 16:24.

CHAPTER 12

Messianic Jewish Identity

Now that we have articulated our understanding of the Torah's goal and the origins of the Oral Law, a very important question remains: Is there a need for distinct messianic Jewish identity in the church? If we answer yes to this question, two other questions follow. First, how does the Law relate to messianic Jewish identity? Second, how do the traditions of our people relate to messianic Jewish identity? Providing comprehensive answers to these questions would require more than even a series of books could deliver. At the same time, these questions demand answers.

Israel Rejected?

"Israel" is one of the most uniting themes in the Bible, mentioned more than 2,500 times. Israel is obviously an important topic to God. Israel's continued existence is guaranteed in the Tanakh,[1] and God's unwavering commitment to his promises concerning Israel is assured in the New Testament.[2] God did not send Yeshua to the

---

1. "Thus says the LORD, who gives the sun for light by day and the fixed order of the moon and the stars for light by night, who stirs up the sea so that its waves roar—the LORD of hosts is his name: 'If this fixed order departs from before me, declares the LORD, then shall the offspring of Israel cease from being a nation before me forever'" (Jer. 31:35–36).

2. "As regards the gospel, they are enemies for your sake. But as regards election, they are beloved for the sake of their forefathers. For the gifts and the calling of God are irrevocable" (Rom. 11:28–29).

world to abolish a distinct Jewish identity, but to "confirm the prom-ises given to the patriarchs" (Rom. 15:8).

Israel's ongoing existence is a certainty; moreover, a physically identifiable remnant of Jewish believers in Yeshua is a theological imperative. Paul makes this quite clear in Romans 11:1–6:

> I ask, then, has God rejected his people? By no means! For I myself am an Israelite, a descendant of Abraham, a mem-ber of the tribe of Benjamin. God has not rejected his people whom he foreknew. Do you not know what the Scripture says of Elijah, how he appeals to God against Israel? "Lord, they have killed your prophets, they have demolished your altars, and I alone am left, and they seek my life." But what is God's reply to him? "I have kept for myself seven thousand men who have not bowed the knee to Baal." So too at the present time there is a remnant, chosen by grace. But if it is by grace, it is no longer on the basis of works; otherwise grace would no longer be grace (Rom. 11:1–6).

Paul forces himself to ask a question that causes him revulsion. "I ask, then, has God rejected his people? By no means!" How can God reject Israel? For Paul, that would be like God rejecting his own char-acter, since the "gifts and the calling of God are irrevocable" (Rom. 11:29). But what proof can Paul offer that God has not rejected Israel, particularly since so many Israelites in his day had rejected God and his Messiah? Paul offers three proofs.

The first is himself: "For I myself am an Israelite, a descendant of Abraham, a member of the tribe of Benjamin." If God still accepts Paul, an Israelite, than clearly he did not reject Israel.

For the second, Paul appeals to the Scripture: "Do you not know what the Scripture says?" Paul's point is simple. If Christians come to the conclusion that God has rejected Israel, they obviously do not know the Scriptures.

For the third, Paul points to the remnant of Jewish believers in Yeshua as proof that God has not rejected Israel. "So too at the present time there is a remnant, chosen by grace" (11:5). As long as there are Jewish believers in Yeshua, there is tangible proof that God has not rejected Israel. An ongoing, tangible remnant of Jewish followers of Yeshua is an essential expression of God's perfect faithfulness.

What Is a Jew?

Before we can provide a definition of a messianic Jew, we must first define who is a Jew. The answer to this question is clearly not tied to the Law for the simple fact that most Jews in the world, including Jews in Israel, are not religious—that is, they do not keep those aspects of the Law that are still possible to keep without the temple. What makes a secular Jew a Jew? The answer is easy: ancestry. A Jew is someone who is a physical descendant of Abraham, Isaac, and Jacob.[3] Therefore, anyone who is of physical descent from Abraham, Isaac, and Jacob and a follower of Yeshua is part of the remnant concerning which Paul testified (i.e., a messianic Jew).

Does following the Law and the Jewish traditions make a Jewish follower of Yeshua more Jewish? Perhaps we can answer the question by asking another question: Does eating Chinese food make a Chinese person more Chinese? The answer is clear: No! Keeping the Law and the Jewish traditions does not make a Jewish believer more Jewish. A Jewish follower of Yeshua is Jewish because of his or her physical ancestors, and this physical heritage and identity provides tangible testimony to the church that God has not rejected Israel.

A reader may easily take our argument further than we intend. We (the authors) are Jewish; we worship on Saturday; we celebrate the biblical feasts; we enjoy *kabbalat Shabbat*;[4] we recite the *shema*[5] in our messianic congregation; and we raise our children in the knowledge of being a part of our people Israel. It is important to explain the reasons why we do these things. We do *not* celebrate the feasts or follow

---

3. Rabbinic Judaism traces Jewish identity through the mother, though the Torah casts some ambivalence on the identity of the son of an Israelite woman (see Lev. 24:11). During the Holocaust, anyone who had at least one Jewish grandparent was considered Jewish enough to be murdered along with the rest of the Jewish people. Therefore, the modern state of Israel allows anyone with one Jewish grandparent to obtain citizenship under the Law of Return.

4. Traditional Friday evening ceremony and meal that welcomes the Sabbath.

5. "Hear, O Israel: The LORD our God, the LORD is one" (Deut. 6:4).

some of the traditions of our people out of a sense of obligation either to the Sinai covenant or to the rabbis.

Messianic Jewish Identity and the Law and Traditions

The book of Hebrews, as we have seen, is quite clear that the new covenant is a *new*, not a *renewed* covenant. Some argue that the circumcised heart in Deuteronomy 30:6 provides divine enablement to keep the Sinai covenant. Likewise, others argue that the new covenant in Jeremiah is a *renewed* covenant whereby God writes the Law of the Sinai covenant in the hearts of his people. There are a number of reasons we believe these conclusions are problematic.

First, Moses intentionally alludes to Israel's experience at Mount Sinai in Deuteronomy 30 in order to contrast this "commandment" with the earlier one.

> For this commandment that I command you today is not too hard for you, neither is it far off. It is not in heaven, that you should say, "Who will ascend to heaven for us and bring it to us, that we may hear it and do it?" Neither is it beyond the sea, that you should say, "Who will go over the sea for us and bring it to us, that we may hear it and do it?" But the word is very near you. It is in your mouth and in your heart, so that you can do it. (Deut. 30:11–14)

"Who will ascend to heaven" is an allusion to Moses going up Mount Sinai to receive the Ten Commandments. "Who will go over the sea for us" is an allusion to Moses bringing the Israelites across the Red Sea to receive the Law. "That we may hear it and do it" is clearly an allusion to Israel's vow at Mount Sinai that they would keep the Law (Exod. 24:7). "Neither is it far off" is an allusion to the people who stood at a distance when Moses went up to receive the commandments at Mount Sinai (Exod. 20:18, 21; 24:1). In other words, this passage anticipates a commandment (covenant) that will be completely different from the commandment of Mount Sinai. This commandment will be internalized (in your mouth and in your heart), that is, written on the circumcised heart (Deut. 30:6), unlike the commandments of Mount Sinai, which are inscribed on stone.

Remarkably, an ancient Jewish-Aramaic paraphrase of this passage understands this to be a reference to the coming of the prophet like Moses (spoken of in Deut. 18:15, 18–19; 34:10): "The Torah is not in the heavens, saying, 'O that we had one like Moses the prophet who would go up to heaven and take it for us, that he might make us hear the commandments so that we would do them'" (Deut. 30:12; *Targum Neofiti*, English translation, Accordance Bible Software). Paul's citation of this passage, likewise, contrasts this commandment (a righteousness by faith in the Messiah Yeshua) with the righteousness that comes through the Law (Rom. 10:4–10). Paul's comments on Deuteronomy 30 make it very clear that the apostle does not understand it to be a renewal of the Sinai covenant but a different covenant altogether.

Second, those who argue that Jeremiah's new covenant is a renewed covenant based on the phrase "I will put my law within them," reading the word "law" to refer to Torah, must contend not only with the clear words of the prophet: "not like the covenant that I made with their fathers" (Jer. 31:32), but also with the unmistakably clear teachings of the Epistle to the Hebrews: "in speaking of a new covenant, he makes the first one obsolete" (Heb. 8:13).

Yeshua's priestly service requires a new covenant—a completely new covenant—a covenant that provides true and eternal cleansing from impurity and sin in the heavenly temple, the provision of which is simply not possible under the Sinai covenant.

The first reason we live our lives in close interaction with the Law and with our traditions is because we are Jewish believers in Yeshua who live among our people in the land of Israel, where Law and tradition shape the everyday lives of our culture and society. By close interaction, we mean that we must critically engage with our traditions, and at times we must reject traditions that go against the Scriptures. At the same time, we are reminded of the testimony of the apostle Paul who insisted time and time again that he "had done nothing against our people or the customs of our fathers" (Acts 28:17; see Acts 25:8, 10). As Paul argues, the Messiah "became a servant to the circumcised to show God's truthfulness, in order to confirm the promises given to the patriarchs" (Rom. 15:8). We live as servants among our people in order to confirm the promises to our fathers.

The second reason we live in close interaction with the Law and our traditions is in order to make the Messiah Yeshua real and understandable to our people. Our people will not understand who Yeshua is in the context of Christmas trees and Easter bunnies. They do, however, value Sabbath rest, Passover redemption, the solemnity of the Day of Atonement, and the beauty of kindled lights. In this context, Yeshua no longer appears like Joseph disguised as an Egyptian, but as Joseph revealed as our brother.

Moreover, not only do the feasts of God point to the Messiah Yeshua, but many of these feasts and holidays also look back to tangible expressions of God's dealings with our people. Passover is our independence day. Sabbath is our reminder that we are no longer slaves in Egypt. Purim is a reminder that the Hamans of this world cannot prevail. We as Jews celebrate the feasts and holidays as a remembrance of God's goodness to our people in the past; in addition, we celebrate these days as tokens of what God will do for our people in the future.

There is no one-size-fits-all messianic Jewish identity. Each Jewish believer lives before the Lord and must live out their faith in a manner that communicates to a dying world, both Jewish and Gentile, that Yeshua is the Messiah. The messianic Jewish world is, in fact, a microcosm of the Jewish world as a whole, with all its complex diversity. May God give us grace and wisdom to seek out ways to shine the light of the Messiah to our people and to the watching world!

Conclusion and Final Challenge

"For the goal at which the Torah aims is the Messiah, who offers righteousness to everyone who trusts" is how the *Complete Jewish Bible* puts Romans 10:4. We have looked at the Torah from various angles to show how its theology is thoroughly messianic and clearly points to the new covenant. We have seen how the Torah story already anticipates a broken Sinai covenant, and looks beyond the thundering mountain to the glorious promises of blessing through the Messiah who will come "in the last days." Since the Torah's goal is to lead us *through* Sinai's broken covenant and *to* the Messiah in the last days, we have been forced to redefine Torah observance as it is typically understood. True Torah observance for the believer today is not to live under the authority of the Law (or the Oral Law), but to believe in Yeshua; for if we believe Moses, we will most certainly believe in Yeshua (John 5:46). We have also looked at the Law—the commandments of the Sinai covenant—and argued that it continues to function as inspired Scripture. The Law witnesses against us, points us to Yeshua, teaches us about God, offers us wisdom and insight, deepens our understanding of the person and work of Yeshua, and challenges us to love God and our neighbor. We have seen how followers of Messiah Yeshua are in the truest sense faithful disciples of Moses, who fulfill the requirements of the Law by believing God and loving people (1 John 3:23).

Finally, we leave you with a challenge: Be consumed with Yeshua, not with laws and traditions! Why? There are two reasons. First, because Moses wrote the Torah to lead us to Yeshua and the new covenant. "Now Moses was faithful in all God's house as a servant, to testify to the things that were to be spoken later" (Heb. 3:5). Second, because lasting change comes only through Yeshua and not through laws or traditions. Yeshua's commandments deal not only with the externals but also with the internal in that they go deep into our hearts and cause us to change through the empowerment of the Holy Spirit. With Yeshua, murder is not limited to a physical slaying—it is a matter of the heart; adultery is not limited to a physical union—it is a matter of the heart. Yeshua calls and empowers us through his Spirit to control our anger, to shun lust, and to love our enemies, all of which would be impossible without outside help. You see, following traditions or concentrating on what and how to do (or not do) external things only embitters us to those around us and causes us to turn against those who do not agree with us.

As we continue to meditate on the riches of the Torah, may we, like David, desire its teachings more "than gold, even much fine gold." May it be to us "sweeter also than honey and drippings of the honeycomb" (Ps. 19:10). As we read the Torah may our eyes be opened to its singular story, whose goal is to restore a lost blessing to humanity through Yeshua, the Messiah-King, whose new covenant frees us to "owe no one anything, except to love each other, for the one who loves another has fulfilled the law" (Rom. 13:8).

Bibliography and Recommended Reading

Alexander, Desmond T. *From Paradise to the Promised Land: An Introduction to the Pentateuch*, 3rd ed. Grand Rapids: Baker, 2012.

Bahnsen, Greg L., ed. *Five Views on Law and Gospel*. Grand Rapids: Zondervan, 1996.

Brown, Michael L. *Answering Jewish Objections to Jesus*. Vol. 5. San Francisco: Purple Pomegranate Productions, 2009.

Clements, R. E. *God and Temple*. Oxford: Basil Blackwell, 1965.

Copan, Paul. *Is God a Moral Monster? Making Sense of the Old Testament God*. Grand Rapids: Baker, 2011.

Dempster, Stephen G. *Dominion and Dynasty: A Theology of the Hebrew Bible*. Downers Grove, IL: InterVarsity Press, 2003.

Gruber, Daniel. *Rabbi Akiba's Messiah: The Origins of Rabbinic Authority*. Hanover, NH: Elijah, 1999.

Guthrie, George H. *Hebrews*. NIV Application Commentary. Grand Rapids: Zondervan, 1998.

Kaiser, Walter C., Jr. *The Messiah in the Old Testament*. Grand Rapids: Zondervan, 1995.

Keil, C. F., and F. Delitzsch. "Ezekiel, Daniel." Vol. 9 of *Commentary on the Old Testament*. Peabody, MA: Hendrickson, 1996.

Meyer, Jason C. *The End of the Law: Mosaic Covenant in Pauline Theology*. Nashville: B&H, 2009.

Morales, L. Michael. *Tabernacle Prefigured: Cosmic Mountain Ideology in Genesis and in Exodus*. Leuven: Peeters, 2012.

Postell, Seth D. *Adam as Israel*. Eugene, OR: Pickwick, 2011.

Rydelnik, Michael. *The Messianic Hope: Is the Hebrew Bible Really Messianic?* Nashville: B&H, 2010.

Rydelnik, Michael, ed. *The Moody Handbook of Messianic Prophecy*. Chicago: Moody, forthcoming.

Sailhamer, John H. *The Pentateuch as Narrative: A Biblical-Theological Commentary*. Grand Rapids: Zondervan, 1992.

_____. *The Meaning of the Pentateuch: Revelation, Composition, and Interpretation*. Downers Grove, IL: InterVarsity Press, 2009.

Satterthwaite, Philip E., Richard S. Hess, and Gordon J. Wenham, eds. *The Lord's Anointed: Interpretation of Old Testament Messianic Texts*. Eugene, OR: Wipf & Stock, 1995.

Schreiner, Thomas R. *40 Questions About Christians and Biblical Law*. Grand Rapids: Kregel, 2010.

_____. *The Law and Its Fulfllment: A Pauline Theology of Law*. Grand Rapids: Baker, 1993.

Thompson, Alden. *Who's Afraid of the Old Testament God?* Grand Rapids: Zondervan, 1988.

Todd, James M., III. *Sinai and the Saints: Reading Old Covenant Laws for the New Covenant Community*. Downers Grove, IL: InterVarsity Press, 2017.

Van Seters, John. "Author or Redactor?" *Journal of Hebrew Scriptures* 7, no. 9 (2007): 1–23.

_____. *The Edited Bible: The Curious History of the "Editor" in Biblical Criticism*. Winona Lake, IN: Eisenbrauns, 2006.

Westerholm, Stephen. *Perspectives Old and New on Paul: The "Lutheran" Paul and His Critics*. Grand Rapids: Eerdmans, 2004.

Zahn, Theodor. *Die Anbetung Jesu im Zeitalter der Apostel*. Leipzig: A. Deichert, 1910.